D0112544

Same Here, Sisterfriend

Mostly True Tales of Misadventures in Motherhood

curated by

Holly Mackle

DEXTERITY
NASHVILLE

DEXTERITY

Dexterity, LLC
604 Magnolia Lane
Nashville, TN 37211

Copyright © 2018

All rights reserved. Except as permitted by the US Copyright Act of 1976, no part of this book may be reproduced, distributed, or transmitted without prior written permission from the publisher. For information, please contact info@dexteritycollective.co.

Scripture quotations are from the ESV® Bible (The Holy Bible, English Standard Version®), copyright © 2001 by Crossway, a publishing ministry of Good News Publishers. Used by permission. All rights reserved.

First edition: 2018
10 9 8 7 6 5 4 3 2 1

Printed in the United States of America.

ISBN: 978-0-9983253-4-7 (trade paper)
ISBN: 978-0-9983253-5-4 (eBook)

Book design by Sarah Siegand.
Cover design by EmeraldMade and Kayla Neely.
Illustrations by Greg Jackson.
Interior design elements by Selena Fettig.

For David,

who isn't threatened by
my infinitely superior sense of humor.

You're my favorite.

Table of Contents

Part IV: Kidfriends

Part V: Gotta Be Your Own Friend

Part VI: Sisterfriends

Foreword

When I was pregnant with our son, people told me encouraging stories about logical, rational, reasonable women who had made the transition into motherhood with confident, elegant ease. They seamlessly integrated a baby's needs into their schedules and, at the same time, conducted conference calls while soothing their little ones to sleep and checking the progress of homemade stew simmering on the stove. These women apparently showed no signs of exhaustion on their glowing faces, and they did courageous things like changing out of their pajamas before eleven o'clock in the morning and somehow fitting in a quick workout during naptime. They weren't stressed, they weren't overwhelmed, and their hair was consistently clean and styled.

They were remarkable.

So you can imagine my disappointment when I realized that I was not, in fact, one of them.

Seriously. Here's the one thing I knew mere days after our son made his entrance into the world: "elegant ease" was nowhere in my personal motherhood skill set.

And that skill set didn't magically appear or even slowly evolve as Alex got older, either. Because if anything became increasingly apparent to me as I navigated life with a newborn, then a toddler, then a preschooler, and on and on, it's that I was a train wreck. I was scatterbrained, I was tired, and, I think, more than anything else, I was afraid.

So you know what I did?

I figured out how to pretend.

I mean, I don't want to brag, but I pretended as if it were my day job, y'all. And I think I could have even won some trophies if awards for pretending actually existed (apart from the Oscars, of course, but I digress). As much as I loved (and still love) being a mama, so many aspects of motherhood just flat-out intimidated me—especially the part where you're supposed to bond effortlessly with other moms and get super vulnerable about whatever your parenting/marriage/career challenges happen to be.

Here was my attitude about motherhood-related vulnerability: *Me no likey.*

Clearly, I had a super mature outlook about the whole thing.

But I'm gonna tell you what: over time—and we're talking years, not months—the consistent love and care and all-the-way-realness of other moms I met along the way just completely won me over. I'm talking about my friend Traci, who laughed her head off when I hesitantly told her about an unfortunate Sunday morning incident when three-year-old Alex greeted one of our pastor's wives by slapping her (it was a real high point for me as a parent, I can promise you). I'm talking about my friend Mary Jo, who sympathetically listened when I recounted Alex's refusal to eat black-eyed peas and who, after I wondered out loud if his stubbornness would eventually lead to him being forty-nine and living in our basement, assured me that we were all going to be just fine. I'm talking about my friend Melanie, who was never too busy to listen to my ongoing existential crisis about how to balance my family life and my work life and my writing life all at the same time, preferably in the most effortless, flawless way.

For the record, this never happens. It's better if you know this now.

And I'm talking about my friends Kasey and Stephanie who nod with great understanding when I bemoan a certain fourteen-year-old's inability to throw away empty boxes instead of putting them back on the pantry shelf as if no one would ever notice the aforementioned emptiness, *for the love* . . .

These women have been some of the greatest gifts of my life. Their sincerity, their candor, their humor, their loyalty—just grace upon grace upon grace. And as you carve out some much-deserved time to read this wonderful, funny, all-the-way-real book that you're holding—written by some pretty spectacular women, I might add—my greatest hope is that you'll remember that you don't have to pretend. You don't have to act like you have all the answers.

Because as much as we can be tempted to think that, as moms, the highest priority is that we have it together, here's the real-live truth: it's way more important that we have each other.

After all, who needs elegant ease when you have friends who make you laugh until your bladder totally betrays you?

Enjoy, everybody!

Sophie Hudson
Author of *A Little Salty to Cut the Sweet,*
Giddy Up, Eunice, and the BooMama Blog

Introduction

Hello! You look fun.

"Fun?" you ask. "Do you see my hair? And that I haven't showered in the last thirty-six hours? And this stain of unknown origin here on my yoga pants?"

No, I mean it. You look fun.

"But . . . but . . ."

No more arguments. I see you behind the mommy glaze and the exercise wear that has no intention of making it to the gym. And, whether you realize it or not, sometimes all you need is another person to take notice and remind you that you *are* fun. Who's the person with the emotional capital to do that? A sisterfriend. She's the kind of friend who will both assist you with mastering your breast pump, *and* know when to tell you *not* to sign up to be room mom. She reminds you of someone you've met before—quite probably a piece of your former self, from the days of midnight Walmart runs because "We're out of caramel popcorn" or "I'm bored. Want to roll the guys' cars?"

A sisterfriend is a link to the younger you that you sometimes miss, and though you wouldn't trade one ounce of your new life with kids and crazy and smudgy fingerprints on every surface less than three feet high, she's the nostalgic reminder of a woman who made one sandwich at a time and then ate it all by herself, or poured a cup of coffee and never had to reheat it in the microwave; a woman who had oodles of free hours for all the new friends in the whole wide world.

There's a version of Youthful Carefree Single Girl lingering inside of me too. And I don't miss her all the time, but when the short people who live in my house join forces in mutiny, I really wish she was around. She would probably make a great pirate joke or start an actual pillow fight just to release some toddler aggression over having to eat more than fruit snacks for dinner. She definitely wouldn't get frustrated or yell or dare to have the thought *how did I get here?* She would rest and trust that God is up to something great in this very moment with the Gatorade spilled all over the floor or the suspicion that the lingering stain is, indeed, permanent marker. She would deal with the surrounding chaos gracefully and energetically and with just the right amount of humor.

Once in a while, I'm her—the easygoing mom. But most of the time, I am very much *not* her. That's why I need my sisterfriends. Because when we all join forces, one of us is bound to tap into her lively youthful self and rally the rest of us in a group text chain with just the right mom jeans GIF.

My sisterfriends are so great, I'd love to introduce you. How about we all meet for a girls' weekend in Carmel and get facials and suntans and finally catch up on *This Is Us*? Or let's just pretend we're doing all that as I introduce you to them with this handy . . .

FLOW CHART

So you will have a little backstory before we begin...

I'm **Holly**, repressed creative with more neuroses
than fingers.

Quirks are kind of my "thing." I once tried to trade them
for my sister's thing, which is looking beautiful
and perfectly accessorized all the time,
but, as it turns out, it doesn't work like that.

I go to book club — same one, five-plus years with

Laura
who smells
people's hair

and

Beka
who has no pets

I go to church with

Emily
who is the
Pied Piper of
middle schoolers

and

Abigail
who has too many
children to still be
lawyering

Emily introduced me to

This dashed line represents
the heartbreak of

Caroline
whom I want to be
like when I grow up

Catherine
Who used to go to church
with us but then moved away

(I'm recovering slowly,
thanks for asking)

I love to write with

Cara
who never looks
pregnant until she
turns around, and
then almost
always is

Lindsey
who once wrote
a piece she can
never post

and

Carrie
who loves a good
flow chart

I used to teach high school with

Nicole
who is the real
ringleader of the
Heathers

And I am college best friends with

Pamela
who once got an A -

Same Here, Sisterfriend

There you have it. Seeing these ladies gathered together in flow chart perfection makes me want to give myself a high five, because it took a certain degree of giddy-up to organize us into this litany of laughter (and tears) that you're about to embark on. And this chart, though perfect in form and flawless in function, does no justice to who these women really are, so I'll introduce them American Girl-style before each of their chapters. I can't wait for you to get to know them. They're the kind of women you want at your back. And you know, the older I get, the more I realize having a close circle of sister-friends is not a phenomenon unique to my little corner of the Deep South. Have you got your people? If so, text them right now and tell them how awesome they are. Looking for your people? I hope this book feels like a nudge to make that a priority for yourself. We've got to help keep each other going strong and staying sane. And, by far, the easiest way to do that is to laugh together. *Solidarity, mama.*

And it's not just for friendship; I want to be the kind of mama who can stop at any given moment to be struck by the ridiculous. I want to be the mama who takes time to pause and chuckle (or sigh or weep a little) at the way life is either exceeding or—sometimes within the same hour—falling short of expectations. Because if we don't pause long enough to ask, "How did we get here? To the brink of insanity?" then we're liable to lose a lot more than just the brain cells that left with the breast milk.

I'm not saying it's easy. Jumping off the motherhood treadmill tops the list of things I have a hard time remembering to do, just behind defrosting meat. But we need women in our lives who are willing to reach over and push that gigantic red emergency stop button when we can't do it for ourselves. If you were to meet any of my sisterfriends at, say, the grocery store or KinderMusik, you might be a little tempted to make some assumptions. *Oh, there's the pretty mom,* or *there's the smart mom,* or *the workout mom* . . . And that's why you'll love reading from their hearts. These women blow stereotypes out of the water. They make me feel goofy for even thinking in stereotypes. They make me want to avoid typecasting the trendy mom in front of me in line at the dentist. You know the one: It's 9:00 a.m. and she probably already has dinner going in the slow cooker. Her kids are keeping their hands to themselves and using words like *thank you* and *please*—I think those are Greek terms, maybe Armenian . . . still not sure. I see her, and I want to trip her in her clean, on-trend, sensible-but-adorable mom flats right as she turns away from the receptionist's desk. But my sisterfriends' words make me want to give her the benefit of the doubt, because yes, her kids are holding it together right at this moment, but chances are one of them is going to stick a Cheerio in their ear the second they get into that recently vacuumed minivan. And she will lose it and blow up at her perfectly hair-bowed four-year-old who will burst into tears and say through a glistening pout, "You don't love me." And, well, maybe I've thought about this a little too much.

Ladies, the mama trenches are rough. We've got to surround ourselves with people who keep us lighthearted, people who don't make us cover over the reality of our lives with concealer and foundation worthy of an appearance on *Dancing with the Stars*.

For me, many of those people are members of my Book Club (really known as Wine Club), which meets once a month, and every time I leave for it, I feel that poison dart of mommy guilt over doing something for myself. Alone. Well, with friends, but not with my family, and certainly not with a diaper bag. And I know yanking out that poison dart is not a real problem compared to, say, nuclear armament, or the fact that I will one day have to explain to my children how I know so many Pitbull lyrics, *but still*. The darts, they do fly. And we've got to pull them out for ourselves and our friends. That's why I go to Book Club.

Since everyone in Book Club started having babies, hardly anybody ever actually read the selected book, even when there was the fairy dust of a gold such-and-such sticker prize on the front cover. Forget reading; some people never even bought the book—except for this one magical time when we picked a Mindy Kaling book. The craziest thing happened: everyone read it. Could it be that's all the capacity these mamas had at the moment? Probably. Was it because of the shortness of the chapters? Could be. Or maybe Mindy is the comedic equivalent of a Magnolia Bakery cupcake? Highly likely. Book Club should award a prestigious gold star prize of its own with stickers that say *We Actually Read This One*.

But even if we haven't read past the introduction, we don't let that stop us from filing through the door and cozying up on the couch because we're really coming for one very specific thing we know will happen: we will sit around and crack each other up. We help each other step out from under the burden of always having to have our act together. We will meet off to the side of the trenches, even within reasonable driving distance of the trenches, should husbands send up a flare. And we will laugh. Because that's what our weary hearts need—a little commiseration and a lot of laughter.

As you read these essays, I hope you'll remember that all of these women intimidate the heck out of me in one or twelve ways, and yet somehow, I get to be their friend and write alongside them and know things about them that can't be unknown.

Yes, me. I get to be their friend.

The girl who may or may not have once lost all the spare forks at a fancy banquet luncheon and can never deny that she once looked like . . .

And when we laugh together in the safety of friendship and transparency and mutual respect, I'm reminded just how vital our relationships are. I'm reminded there's not one of us who's really got much figured out. We can all appear as if we're blissfully floating on glassy waters when in reality our little webbed feet are paddling as fast as they can through the undercurrents of our lives. But if we keep doing that, we'll never be truly known—nor ever really know our sisterfriends. And if we're honest with each other about just how hard we're paddling and just how in the depths we often feel, well, we'll only connect our hearts. Transparency breeds transparency, which breeds depth of friendship.

Speaking of, have you ever texted a friend a picture of your messy kitchen? If not, I highly recommend it. In fact, if you've got a messy kitchen right this second, do yourself a favor and put down this book and go snap a shot of it. Then send it to a woman you want to get to know better, long to connect with more frequently, or think is the coolest girl you know. Here, I'll even give you the caption. Write:

So this is happening right now.

I felt like someone should know.

Hit send on that puppy and watch what happens. If you've picked the right girl, she will respond back with an insane amount of laughing emojis, a joke about *Hoarders*, or a pic of her own even messier kitchen. If she responds back with anything less awesome, well, you picked the wrong chick and, if at first you don't succeed, try again.

* * * * *

If I have anything correct in my head about human nature, most moms feel alone and in over their head at some time or another—with questions, doubts, mistakes, and serious regrets, of course along with all the sweet and priceless moments too. We often *feel* alone, don't we, but it just can't possibly be the case that we are. So my lovely friend Lake is very pleased to share a simple craft to help ward off the negative attacks. It's just like Lake to come up with a crafting solution—she always knows where her hot glue gun is. At the mention of a craft, some of you (mostly Lake) just felt your heart flutter, but for the rest of you non-crafties (me), don't fear, I'm here. We can figure this out together. We might have to call a friend for backup, but I think we can handle it. So, let's make a bookmark. You can do this.

Deep breath. Shoulder roll. Knuckle crack.

Okay, turn the page for instructions . . .

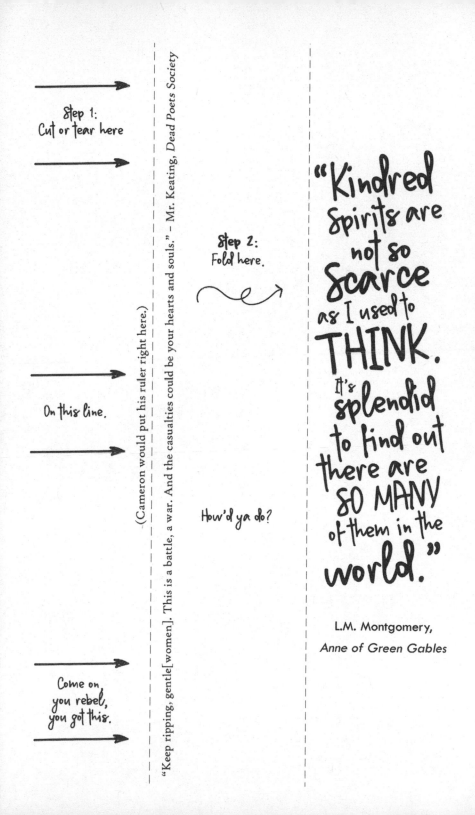

Step 1:
Cut or tear here

On this line.

Come on
you rebel,
you got this.

—(Cameron would put his ruler right here.)

"Keep ripping, gentle[women]. This is a battle, a war. And the casualties could be your hearts and souls." – Mr. Keating, *Dead Poets Society*

Step 2:
Fold here.

How'd ya do?

"Kindred spirits are not so scarce as I used to THINK. It's splendid to find out there are SO MANY of them in the world."

L.M. Montgomery,
Anne of Green Gables

Not so bad, right? Was that cathartic for anyone else? Okay, just me . . . But look how handy it will be to remind you that whichever sisterfriend you're reading has her battles, and you've got yours. The mom in me wants to tell you, "Use your bookmark! Make good choices!" But I won't, I promise. I'll exercise my own self-control and remind myself *we're all grown-up big girls and we can all make our own grown-up big-girl decisions, including whether or not we're going to do the super cute and clever bookmark craft that helps to remind us to go easy on everyone, including ourselves.*

(Tacky, right? Ahem . . . sorry . . .)

But I do hope you'll pull up a chair, get cozy, and get ready to join the flow chart. Laugh at us, laugh with us, and (hopefully) get a little more okay with laughing at yourself.

Part 1
Babyfriends

Pro Tip: Buy more dry shampoo. I mean, is there enough? I keep worrying there's going to be a shortage. I hoard a bottle every time I get a birth announcement.

1
Lactation

Laura Royal

Meet Laura. In her free time, she enjoys making up figure skating routines to whatever song is currently running through her head. Laura hasn't taken figure skating lessons a day in her life, but is a shoe-in to medal in choreography at World Championships.

I got my first of two marriage proposals when I was six. I was making a perfectly arched stair step rainbow with my Legos, and with smooth skills like that, who could blame Britt Smitherman for wanting to make me his own? Unfortunately, we both had too much baggage and the engagement didn't last. But I look back at that season of life fondly, because it turns out that's pretty much the only time I've been ahead of schedule on anything. Since then, I've been on the tail end of things for most of my seasons of life.

It took two careers to find the one that would stick, which came when I was thirty. My second (and thankfully more meaningful) engagement and subsequent marriage came when I was thirty-eight. I had my first child at forty-one and my second at forty-three. Now, at forty-seven, I finally diffused my first essential oil, but I still haven't downloaded the Pandora app. Suffice it to say, I'm consistently doing "my thing," whatever it is, at least a decade behind everyone else. (Did you know you could get the Internet on your phone now? The marvels never cease.)

But there is one area where I turned out to be ahead of my time. I discovered it after my first daughter was born, and it was confirmed again after her younger sister arrived. Simply put, I was a spectacularly above-average lactator—a real blue-ribbon Holstein.

Yep, that's right. The girls sure could make some milk, easily filling eight-ounce storage bags that lined up in my freezer, row after glorious row, like rectangular white pillars of overachievement. I had enough milk to make me look for deep freezers on Craigslist, no longer concerned that the previous owners had used them to store pork casings and venison. I had enough to make me forget all the times I saw "**ADVANCED MATERNAL AGE!**" proclaimed on my medical chart. Okay, so maybe it wasn't written in boldface capitals. And maybe there wasn't actually an exclamation point at the end, either. Maybe I just felt really tired and my feet hurt and for nine months I felt old, and *that's* what I'm remembering. My point is that any time you are being exceptional at something, you just want to celebrate it, right?! And freeze it! And make wagers with your friends about whether or not you can hit the gallon mark in less than twenty-four hours! Lactation really pumped me up. Bad pun celebrated.

Lactation

I know lots of new moms don't love breastfeeding or pumping, and I can definitely see why, with all the cracking and bleeding and leaking and blocked ducts, not to mention walking around with nursing pads in your bra, like some weird throwback to when you stuffed it in seventh grade. But in two words, here's the reason lactating like a boss is awesome: Lactation Center. I work at a large hospital that has the most *amazing* employee Lactation Center you have ever seen. Trust me, using it is like taking a mini-vacation at work. There is a really comfortable chair with a remote and a flat-screen TV mounted on the wall at eye level with all the channels you could ever want to watch. And the shiny new state-of-the-art pump apparatus is set so all you have to do is plug in your tubing and watch the magic happen. Except that you aren't watching the magic happen, you are watching Rachael Ray in high-definition, wondering how anyone could ever be so genuinely excited about kale, while eating your Lean Cuisine on an ergonomic table. I'm telling you, the Lactation Center is a destination among destinations, a gentle front hug for you and your overworked, underappreciated bosom.

On my inaugural visit to the Lactation Center, it was my first day back at work and my baby was twelve weeks old. Up to that point I had been using my consignment sale pump (affectionately called Old Yeller) at home like a pro, and had really grown to love it. Its worn-out carrying case and now useless Velcro strips felt like an old friend. So when I went back to work,

5

I was already aware of my super-stellar overachiever milking abilities. I giddily went into one of the four stalls, which was a six-by-eight-foot space separated from the others by a wooden partition stretching about three-quarters of the way to the ceiling on either side and a curtain to pull closed behind me. If Pottery Barn, Best Buy, and Mr. Clean all had a love child, it would be this space. The shiny hardwood floors, plush leather chair, wooden partitions, and privacy curtain were all varying shades of neutrals and browns. Not browns that depress you, but browns that *soothe* you, like summer camp, and make you want to get your latest guilty pleasure and curl up and forget whatever it is you are supposed to be doing—for weeks.

So I got myself all situated, found my girl Rachael Ray, and started to pump. Soon, more women came in and the other three stalls were filled. As we all sat there, the rhythmic sound of the pumping became louder and louder. Or maybe I was fiddling with the remote and I might have accidentally muted my TV. Suddenly all I could hear was everyone's pumping cadence, and all I could picture was a barn full of cows getting milked. This is what sleep deprivation does to you: it takes away your filter. So there in the Lactation Center, without a follow-up plan, I did it. I mooed. Actually, I *moooooeeeed.*

It was uncomfortably long.

And loud.

I actually did it twice.

To my surprise, I got crickets both times.

I had to make sure that the other pumpers heard me and that they got the joke, because we are all milking, right? It's funny! Solidarity, my Medela sisters! We Pump In Style®! So I leaned in the direction of the other stalls, and loudly explained to everyone, "I mooed, because we are all being like cattle right now, with our pumping . . . do y'all get it? That's why you heard the sound. Of the mooing."

Finally one of my fellow pumpers, who probably felt sorry for me being a newbie and all, mercifully responded, "We hear you, baby. You just keep on going in there." I'm pretty sure that's lactation code, loosely translated as: "Just be quiet and watch your awesome flat-screen, bless your heart. And maybe also quit referring to us as cattle."

It would be an awesome ending to the story if I had come out to find that it was my boss's boss in there who heard me moo, or maybe some fringe co-worker I was going to have to see every day until retirement. And maybe it was. But I'll never know, because I hunkered down in my milking stall and waited until I heard everyone leave. And I could tell when that happened, because the Lactation Center also has a *microwave where you can sterilize your pump parts before you leave!* I know, right?!? After the final beep indicated I was free to go, I skulked out of that Lactation Center like a vegan out of Chick-fil-A. Lesson learned: not everyone is going to be as enthusiastic as

you are to draw parallels between pumping hour and bovine traffic control.

In the end, I didn't care, because I never even *saw* my lactating sistren, and even if I did, who's to say that the ill-timed moo was even from me? Maybe someone's Medela Pump In Style® malfunctioned, or maybe someone had their flat-screen on Animal Planet during "Sickly Livestock Week." All I know is that I can still build a breathtaking symmetrical rainbow with Legos, and my husband says he will download Pandora onto my phone and even customize it for me, so really there's not much else I need to prove to anyone. So that's it, I'm plugging right along on my own growth curve.

But Britt Smitherman, if you're out there, thanks for the memories. You completed me, in a kindergarten kind of way. As a show of my gratitude, I have a gently used deep freezer for you; let me know when you can pick it up.

2
The Diaper Fiasco:
a Case Study in Mommy Legalism
Pamela Wells

Meet Pamela. If you're looking for a friend who once scared a guy away on a first date by asking him about his views on the Sabbath, she's your gal. But she can't be your BFF. I called dibs in '99.

My daughter turned fifteen months old and I needed a night off. A group of friends had booked reservations at one of those wine-and-painting classes, and I was counting down the minutes. Thankfully, my loving, supportive husband was fully capable of tackling the bedtime routine on any given night. Unbeknownst to him, this would be no ordinary night.

But first, let's back up a few hours. That morning while my husband was at work, I embarked on a mission of altruism—a feat of magnanimity for all creation: I bought hybrid diapers for my

daughter. These diapers had a washable fabric shell, a leak-resistant plasticky liner, and a flushable, even compostable insert. No longer would I be part of the bourgeois masses who contribute mindlessly to the growing landfill problem! I would be restoring precious nutrients to the earth's soil! It made no difference to me that I had no access to composting facilities in my second-story apartment—I could still *theoretically* do it. And that made me feel like the Queen of Green. Somewhere, Captain Planet stood akimbo in his high red boots and nodded his authoritative approval.

Perhaps you wonder why I felt the burden to take such a step in the name of environmental heroism? That's a good question, and I've had some time to think about it. Let's start with my upbringing. Culturally, I'm a daughter of the women's lib generation, trained to believe I could do it all and have it all. Raised on the meat-and-potatoes of achievement, I had just enough privilege, encouragement, and propaganda to embrace as fact that I could—and must—achieve my way to a replete and fulfilling personhood. I was the master of my own destiny, and if I wasn't mastering something, then surely I was being ungrateful for the opportunities afforded me by not living up to my potential for success. I embraced this ethos with gusto, even as a Christian whose identity, by definition, was found in God's grace rather than my own achievement. The other factor is, of course, my own nature. As a student, I always strove for likability and academic excellence. As a career woman, I continued to strive for likability and professional excellence.

Then motherhood hit.

Likability? This baby screams in my face and throws food at me! No one has ever treated me like that. In my previous life, she would have been fired or put on academic probation. *Excellence*? I don't know what the heck I'm doing most of the time. I'm never going to find where she put her shoes. And are you telling me that the "grade" for my success in raising this child won't come for another twenty years? I can't handle that! Achievement addicts need more frequent hits. Time for grasping: enter hybrid diapers, followed by a list of other action steps. Switch to all-natural bathroom cleaner so my baby's bottom never touches the residue of Clorox? Check. Make my own baby food to protect my child from a tinge of BPA that could be lingering in that jar lid? Check. Between the spit-ups and the failed naps and the loss of regular showering, mama's gotta achieve something. So give me a flash of inspiration and two-day shipping on Amazon Prime, and I'll take on diaper sustainability.

I breezed through my daughter's wet diaper changes throughout the day. The flushing was successful as long as I followed the instructions carefully: the disposable insert needed to be ripped lengthwise in order to avoid clogging the toilet. This was especially important due to the fifty-year-old plumbing in our building. But overall, things went so swimmingly that I altogether forgot to mention to my husband that I'd switched from regular disposables to hybrid diapers before I left for my night out. Oops!

And, that morning, I tucked our remaining disposables away to save for traveling and laundry emergencies. I grabbed my purse and headed out for what promised to be a carefree night.

If you've never been to one of those wine-and-painting classes, I highly recommend it. With a group of friends, a glass of Pinot, fist-pumping hits from the nineties, and step-by-step painting instruction, I can produce a pretty darn acceptable imitation of Van Gogh. My outing was just what this busy, and sometimes lonely, mother needed. I painted and laughed and caught up with good friends without a thought of concern over my baby and husband. After all, I had my cell phone with me, and surely he'd call if there was an emergency. The only thing I hadn't considered was the unlikelihood of hearing my phone while buried in my purse hanging on the wall behind me over the chatter of friends and blaring tunes.

When the painting class was over, I checked my phone and found that I had missed at least eight texts and calls from my husband. And there was a clear progression of exasperation.

"Hey, are we using new diapers?"

"Hey, she pooped. Can you call me quickly to explain these diapers?"

"I tried to flush this insert, but the toilet is clogged."

Then three or four missed calls followed by, "WILL YOU PLEASE ANSWER? THE BATHROOM IS FLOODED."

I knew then and there that I would not be lingering to chat in the parking lot with friends or greeted by a sweet kiss and a

"Did you have fun, babe?" when I got home. When I arrived, I walked through the door with the posture and facial expression of sheepish guilt. I apologized profusely and listened to my husband recount the diaper fiasco with color in his cheeks. Our daughter had blown out the hybrid and he hadn't been able to find the old disposable diapers. He'd tried to flush the insert from the dirty diaper, but since he hadn't followed the crucial ripping step, the toilet had clogged. When he tried to flush again, the toilet began to run over onto the bathroom floor. All this went on while our daughter lay bare-bottomed on the bedroom floor because he wasn't sure how to assemble a fresh diaper. He eventually got her diapered and put to bed, but he was *not* happy.

From distinguished Queen of Green to humbled Careless Wife and Culpable Accessory to Home Flooding in the course of a few hours, my achievement-centered identity was reeling. I immediately started an internal dialogue of self-justification. First, I turned to nineties nostalgia—not for the music I had enjoyed at the painting studio, but for the days before the ubiquity of cell phones. *Remember those days when we weren't expected to be available by cell phone at any given moment? What did husbands do back then? They just had to deal with it, right? I miss those days.* Next, I turned to man-bashing thoughts: *If I'd been home alone, I'd have to figure it out on my own. Why do men expect that the mother can magically solve any baby-related problem? Do I call him at work whenever I have a problem with the baby? No!*

Finally, I turned to more detached, simplistic defenses: *I'm not a plumber—how could I have helped?* But deep down, I knew I had just blown it. My husband hadn't suffered this fiasco because he was clueless or incompetent—anyone who hadn't read the instruction manual would have missed the crucial insert-ripping step that led to the flooding. As much as I was tempted to blame-shift, his frustration with me was valid.

So I found myself at one of those crucial existential junctions. It was a painful moment where my addiction to (and maybe even worship of) achievement contrasted with my profession of faith in, and dependence on, Jesus. Could I accept that Jesus loved and accepted me even if my husband was still deeply frustrated with me? Even if I had failed to be the perfect mom who has it all together? Could I accept that I was loved and safe with Jesus even if my eco-diaper program had gone bust and my bathroom had flooded? And even if—who knows—my baby had consumed some Red Dye #40? Most importantly, could I accept that Jesus is lovingly patient with me through my ongoing struggle with achievement addiction?

Slowly, the death of achievement-centered identity became sweet. It opened the door to the inner freedom and rest that every mom truly needs, more than nights out or babysitters or getaway weekends. So I'll raise my glass—with fear and trembling—to diaper fiascos; to spit-up and ruined naps and missed showers; to failed attempts at eco-friendly righteousness and mommy legalism. Because at the end of the night, I still had paint under my fingernails and a Van Gogh imitation to hang on my wall, reminding me that mess and beauty are friends.

3
Chestnut, Party of Two

Catherine Chestnut

Meet Catherine. In December 2006, she changed her last name from Branch to Chestnut and regrets being married in an era before the wedding hashtag. We've got your back, Catherine. #ChestnutsStrollingDownTheAisle #WhenTheTreeBecomesANut

---

When it came to the delivery of our twins, my ob-gyn Dr. C told us she didn't like to go beyond thirty-eight or thirty-nine weeks before inducing labor. She had no arguments from me. My pregnancy up until that point had been full of the normal aches, pains, and sciatica-inspired waddling, as well as a few unexpected bodily growths, sleeplessness, heart palpitations, varicose veins, and acne in places even teenagers haven't seen. But since all these symptoms put me in the "normal" category, after each routine checkup I was sent home with the proverbial pat on the back. The line became rote: "Keep doing what you're doing," which at that time was chasing around a seventeen-month-old wild man with a weighted beach ball strapped around my midsection. As the pregnancy progressed, I began to fantasize about those two magical little words "bed rest" but instead I got "You look awesome" all the way up to the induction.

As the big day approached, I was instructed not to eat after midnight. So naturally as soon as the clock struck twelve, I was overcome by an insatiable craving for a double bacon cheeseburger. (I don't even like double bacon cheeseburgers.) Per further instructions, my husband and I were asked to check in at the hospital at approximately 3:00 a.m. Therefore, I arrived *extra* hangry and *extra* tired for what promised to be a marathon day.

After the nurses hooked me up to the proper tubes and wiring and had us sign a tree worth of paperwork, they looked at the twins on ultrasound and announced, "Both heads are down! Your conditions look ideal for our easy three-step vaginal delivery process. Would you like an epidural?"

"Can I get a double dose?"

The nurse nodded and said, "The anesthesiologist will be right in."

Up to this point, I've failed to mention one pertinent little detail. By marriage alone, I have a somewhat recognizable last name in the obstetric anesthesia community. In their world, my last name carries the weight of a Kennedy or a Jolie-Pitt. And it became apparent that someone may or may not have mentioned to the anesthesia intern that my last name matched the one on the

Textbook of Obstetric Anesthesiology. He looked at me as though he had been shocked by a stun gun, and I thought, *Yes, you heard right, Rookie. My father-in-law wrote the textbook for the procedure you are about to perform on me, his beloved daughter-in-law. Good luck, partner.*

The intern's hands were trembling when he shook my hand, so I'm guessing they were still trembling when he inserted the gargantuan needle into my spine. And whatever did or did not occur, all I know is that I quickly lost feeling in my legs and abdomen, and then a circus elephant sat on my chest. I guess I received the double dose I requested.

"This doesn't feel right!" I insisted, gasping for breaths, hyperventilation approaching. "My fingers are tingling!"

The nurse oxygen-masked my face and literally pulled the plug from my back. "There you go," the intern said, as his voice cracked. I'll never know if it was because he was nervous or still in the throes of puberty.

"Won't she be needing that?" my husband asked.

"That dose will last her through the delivery and then some," the nurse replied.

"You're sure?" The about-to-be father of twins was still not convinced.

"Yep!" Then the nurse snapped a blue hair net on me and rolled me bed-bound to the surgical room where they hoisted me into position.

"I feel like a paralyzed walrus," I announced to the operating room full of nameless medical personnel, but they seemed
unfazed. They probably heard that kind of thing all the time.

"Are you ready to push?" Dr. C asked as she strolled into the
room, snapping latex gloves against her hands.

I chuckled. *Really?*

I remember clutching tightly onto my husband's upper
arm—partly for the support, but mostly because I wanted him
securely anchored by my head and not sharing the doctor's view.

"One, two, three!" Dr. C counted from between my opened
legs. I released a breath of air, just as she had asked.

"Great!" the doctor exulted with an eye on the contraction
monitor. "Let's get ready to do it again!"

"One, two, three!" And there she was. A long gangly-looking
Twin A—eyes blinking open in the sterile light and looking about
as shocked as I felt when she was transferred to the nurse's waiting
arms. Dr. C quickly turned back to the work that would produce
Twin B. She tucked her hand inside to seek out the second head,
and her wrist disappeared from view.

"I don't feel Twin B," Dr. C announced.

Immediately, the room stilled around me. My husband's
face paled.

*(A quick medical tutorial: When delivering multiples, once the
first baby is delivered, the uterus begins contracting down to
its original size. The other baby or babies must be extracted*

within a certain time frame or they will be suffocated by the contractions. Normally, at this point most doctors would have performed an emergency C-section for the second baby's delivery, meaning I would have had to recover from both a vaginal and C-section delivery.)

But fear not, we had Dr. C, and "C" apparently stands for Cowgirl.

Beware, dear reader: what comes next may defy the mind and cause some subliminal pain. First, her forearm disappeared and then the thicker part of her arm up to her elbow. I've since done the math: approximately one-ninth of her entire person was inside me. You can imagine my distress.

"Twin B has floated to the top of the uterus and is transverse." In plain-speak: the baby was sideways.

Dr. Cowgirl's eyes alternated quickly between the contraction screen and the baby's heart rate monitor. Between contractions, Dr. C would twist and pull and maneuver. Every time my uterus contracted, her arm and the baby were trapped immobile. No one gave me any instructions; my body was doing its own natural work and thanks to the epidural overdose, I couldn't feel the slightest pinky fingernail of the doctor's bodily invasion. *Wherever you are, prepubescent anesthesia intern, thank you!*

Within minutes, Dr. C pulled the second purpled alien out of my body by her heel and Twin B was whisked to a waiting examination station. The room was fairly quiet, and my husband moved toward the bustling swarm of nurses to get a look at our daughters.

"Are they ok?" I asked him, feeling panicked as the doctor continued doing whatever it is they do down there after the babies are out.

My husband turned around with tears in his eyes and said, "They're perfect."

A nurse walked up to my husband and placed a twin in each arm—they were the exact same weight and fit in the length of his forearms. He shook his head and blinked back a few tears before he said, "That was the coolest procedure I've ever seen! I mean, she was up to her elbow inside you!"

Dr. C smiled at the compliment and said to me, "You'll be feeling that later."

She was right. And while newly-minted Dr. Anesthesia intern might have needed a bit of review from the beloved Chestnut family tome, we can't wait to read Dr. Cowgirl's textbook—she's up to her elbows in material.

4
An Abundance of Lack

Beka Rickman

Meet Beka. The Myers-Briggs Type Indicator has yet to officially recognize her preferred personality identity of NOCT, or Non-Outdoorsy Couch Troll. She remains optimistic her marginalized peers will eventually find the motivation to demand proper representation, maybe when they finish their most recent Netflix binge.

"Does it matter what kind of formula I buy or do they all work the same?" I stood in the baby aisle of a Mega Buystuffcheaper, my cell phone glued to my ear with one hand and the other hand on my hip. I was on a mission and had no time for pleasantries. The plan to buy formula would solve all my woes, but I faced being thwarted by a completely unnecessary abundance of options: Sensitive . . . Neocare . . . Soy . . . Organic . . . *Isn't there one for sleep aid? Melatonin care?*

"Well," my friend said very slowly, sensing the snowballing hysteria in my voice, "why *exactly* do you need baby formula?"

"Because I haven't slept in *months*. Because my daughter has never *once* taken a bottle, even though I have pumped enough breast milk to warrant a flood advisory. Because she will not swallow a single bite of baby food. Because I want to go to a movie theater or a restaurant or a dentist appointment without receiving a panic text from the sitter that my baby isn't eating, and I. Am. Over. It." There is a small chance that my voice had risen, ever so slightly, as I tried to explain my situation.

I called this friend because I knew that she had formula-fed all her children and was one of the best moms I knew. I respected her and trusted her. And although she was a great supporter and advocate of breastfeeding mothers, she had been unable to breastfeed her own children for more than a few weeks. If she could be a great mom and not get stuck being a human vending machine then *so could I!* I also chose this friend because I knew she wouldn't judge me for what I considered to be giving up.

"Ok," she said calmly, in a tone you would use with a skittish horse. "I'm not going to tell you not to buy the formula."

"Good!" I retorted.

"However, I *am* going to tell you, based on my own personal experience, that regardless of what your daughter eats, she's still going to need you. She's still going to need you every day. And every night. For years and years and years and years. And what she eats isn't going to change that."

With a great sigh, I told her I'd call her back later and got off the phone. I didn't want her to hear me cry. I hung my head, closed my eyes, and lost it right in the middle of the store. The tower of thirty-dollar formula cans rose above me like an idol I had made to the moms who I thought had it "easier" than me. I felt the teardrops hit the tops of my shoes. Some Mega Buystuffcheaper employees made their way back to the break room, and I didn't even care if they stared at me or if I looked crazy. I cried and cried. Then I shuffled to the front of the store with puffy red eyes and bought a candy bar and drove home to nurse my daughter to sleep.

From the quiet of our rocking chair, I realized my distress wasn't about what my daughter ate. It wasn't that she wanted to nurse all night and never sleep in her own bed; it was that I felt I had nothing left to give. I wanted to give her the world. I wanted to engage and nourish and soothe. I wanted to be enough for her, but my friend's words from earlier helped me realize I would never be enough for her. And that was okay, because she needed me anyway.

I think that when you see the innocence of children, the way they gaze at you with unconditional love and acceptance, you truly begin to see the cracks in your own towers, the feebleness in your own love. You will never be enough, yet they will love and need you anyway.

My new reality made me think of my dependence on God and how His love and strength are limitless. I think this is important to remember, because if our children don't see our weaknesses, how will they see that God is there and willing to help?

If they don't see our lack, how will they learn of His abundance?

If they don't learn of our failures, how will we teach them of His successes?

God is the only perfect parent, and we are not Him. We never will be. But we can rest assured that He delights in using our imperfect love as a way to point our kids to the One who *is* love. Perfect, reliable, never-changing love. For this, I am grateful.

5
Baggage

Abigail Avery

Meet Abigail. She loves a good conference and can rap every lyric to Young MC's "Bust A Move." Yes, I knew we would be friends from the moment we met.

My four-year-old asked to touch my face the other day and reached out her hand to caress the skin under my eyes. I asked her what she was doing and she innocently replied, "Feeling your bags, Mama." Of course. Naturally. Humility dose, *check*. Later that afternoon, I glanced in a mirror and realized she was right. I hadn't slept through the night in two weeks and while caffeine was managing to keep my eyes open, it clearly wasn't covering up my resemblance to a Zero Meth billboard. *Yikes*, I thought, and grabbed the concealer. After a few minutes, two makeup brushes, and lots of blending, I felt I had achieved marginal victory. I began wondering though, *When did this happen? When did concealer cease to exist exclusively for zits and get repurposed for anti-aging superpowers? Did it coincide with the year Jennifer Aniston got the spokesperson job for the Aveeno Ageless™ line?*

This reverse metamorphosis couldn't have happened overnight. It must have been a slow, eroding, carving-of-the-Grand-Canyon process, initiated sometime after that first baby. There's nothing like adjusting to sleeping in microintervals to induce the beginning of crow's-feet and under eye puffiness. Not to mention the complete lifestyle overhaul that goes along with becoming a parent—the never-ending nursery rhyme soundtrack, miasma of spit-up clinging to every item of clothing you own, and the basic restructuring of life as you know it. Which brings me to another kind of bag that seems to materialize when you have kids: the diaper bag. Before our first child was born, I would have naively suggested diaper bags were for diapers, and maybe some goldfish. I had not yet been informed that even a simple trip to the grocery store could feel like the seventh circle of Dante's inferno. First, I'd need to find real clothes to wear, and at that point, pants with zippers openly mocked me from my closet. Then there was all the gear: bottles, wipes, more wipes, extra clothes, a thermometer, Tylenol (in case fever struck in the freezer section), all the pacifiers (and I mean *all* of them), a burp cloth, the softer burp cloth, a bib, educational and age-appropriate toys, sanitizing wipes for said toys, and three pairs of socks. Oh, and some diapers.

Of course, as one grocery trip morphed into the next and I figured out how to fill the grocery bags while keeping my daughter *in* the cart, I became more comfortable. I didn't break out in a sweat if a long checkout line prevented us from being home at exactly one o'clock for her afternoon nap. My type A personality was making progress. I was *rocking* this parenting thing. Of course, my single-kid righteousness was in desperate need of a reality check, and about that time, our son was born.

To preface, I love him so much. But I cannot adequately express how much, how loud, and how often he screamed. I was convinced he was broken. Gradually, and entirely because of nothing I did, he outgrew the fussiness. Meanwhile, my first-born, easy baby (or as a friend describes her first, my "show pony") was falling apart at the seams. Her compliant spirit morphed into that of an attention-seeking, Disney Channel child star on the verge of collapse. She began to throw tantrums like Kanye throws Twitter rants. One time, via video monitor, I caught her deliberately squeezing an entire tube of diaper cream on a wool rug and grinding it into as many fibers as possible with her foot. Later she would justify her misdemeanor with, "Mommy wouldn't let me have another cookie." (Later, while she was safely in time-out and out of sight, I ate the second cookie, because I'm a sinner too and spite felt right. It's a special level of depravity to realize you want to get back at your two-year-old.) Perhaps it was the spite-eating, the excessive diaper-changing, or the value-size jug of carpet cleaner I now owned, but it seemed I was no longer "rocking" this whole parenting thing. The crow's-feet had clawed their way onto my face along with dark rings, which I convinced myself were *shadows*, rain or shine. *Shadows*, I tell you.

And then I was pregnant again. Quick math told me I would be having three kids in four years. My experienced uterus looked full-term at fourteen weeks. What seemed like both a high-speed short and eternally long nine months later, we welcomed our third child and second daughter. I found myself thrilled to welcome another precious life into the world, but was also disproportionately excited about the idea of an extended hospital stay afterward. Packing my bag felt like I was getting ready for vacation. The newly renovated hospital was spa-like and even had a heated toilet seat that did everything except actually pee for me. It was the lap of postpartum luxury, and I asked if I could extend my stay a few nights. Or weeks. I tried to convince myself I wanted to stay because of the amenities, the nurses, and the *quiet*. But really, I had a tremendous fear of coming home with a newborn to the waiting four-year-old and nineteen-month-old. Blue Cross quickly informed me I would be going home on time. So the toilet and I had one last moment before we loaded up to face the entire crew under one roof.

Family, friends, and adrenaline took over for the first several days. About a week later, I was staring down a day alone with all three of my offspring. I tried to anticipate all the challenges that were to come. I really did. I had rotating baskets of toys. I moved all our essentials into one room so everyone would be close. We had two changing tables in a fifteen-hundred-square-foot house, but I hadn't foreseen the need to have extra garbage bags on hand. It started with the baby crying. I spent no less than twenty minutes trying to get her to latch on. She fought me with great fervor considering she was essentially an eight-pound baked potato. I tried to be calm and "relax," just like all the lactation consultants told me, so mentally I went to a beach in St. Lucia, and a few bloodcurdling minutes later we had a nurser! But my dreams of the warm beach were interrupted by the sound of glass shattering. I whipped my head around and saw the nineteen-month-old hanging from the pantry shelves. He had scaled the shelves—in dire and immediate straits of hunger—and knocked a bottle of red wine onto the floor.

"Do. Not. Move!" I shouted as I decided how to proceed and which child I would save: the hungry infant who had just taught us all a lesson about the potential lung capacity of a baked potato, or the glass-shard-endangered toddler? I delicately maneuvered the baby with me over to the pantry to rescue the toddler. I instructed him to stay out of the kitchen until I cleaned it up. After forty-five minutes of watching that wine soak completely into my wood floors, the baby finished eating, and I headed back in there. The stain left no doubt—it was definitely Colonel Mustard in the kitchen with a candlestick.

All of this in the name of breastfeeding. I swept the pieces of glass into a dustpan and then poured them into the trash bag, hearing the delicate clink of pieces as they landed inside—the perfect metaphor for my life as a mom of three in four years. And as my four-year-old stared at me with eyes that were silently pleading, *Please let me off this crazy train and also can I have some more fruit snacks?*, I mourned the fact that I had *no more wine*.

By the time our fourth baby was born, about two-and-a-half years later, I had all but abandoned any illusion that I had things under control. It had been a slow six years of the Lord's undoing of me and my parenting efforts. Each time we brought home a baby, I had prepared as though I was going into battle, all on my own. I wanted to make God proud with the gifts He was entrusting to us. I wanted to present each child as evidence of my hard work as a mom and hear "well done" because of how they behaved or what they achieved.

God doesn't tend to be too subtle with me. We met our new daughter the morning of April 3, Good Friday. We welcomed her new life on the day when we remember Jesus lovingly and obediently giving up His own—the day He laid down His perfection in exchange for my flaws. My daughter's birthday is a sweet reminder that I can never carry all these bags alone. The bags marked mother and wife and friend and daughter—they're all too heavy for me to even fake lifting. And praise God I don't have to.

Perhaps one day, I'll make it far enough on this journey to give up concealer entirely, but I doubt it. I still live in the South, after all, and will see half our town at the grocery store.

Part II
Toddlerfriends

Pro Tip: The finger puppets at the library
will always be at a level of questionable cleanliness.
Say no now so you can say no forever.

6
On Turning Thirty and Driving a Minivan

Caroline Saunders

Meet Caroline. Emily thought she and I would be great writing friends, and as the age-old fairytale goes, modern technology created a friendship between two people who have never actually met in person. (I am almost completely certain she isn't a bot.) Caroline's husband is the spitting image of NFL quarterback Aaron Rodgers, and under just the right haircut conditions, my husband David looks one-sixteenth Brett Favre, so basically Caroline and I are NFL wives and can share all our NFL-wife problems.

I am turning thirty, and I drive a minivan, and this does not depress me whatsoever. I could write sonnets about my minivan. I think I love it more than I love my husband, who can only open one door at a time for me, while the van can open two doors and pop the trunk with the click of a button. Plus, the van actually shielded me from my newest most deep-seated fear: the deranged ostriches with red eyes which attacked us at the nearby safari park. My husband didn't do *anything* except sit there and laugh, so that's it—he's the worst, and the van is the best.

As for turning thirty, the milestone gets a bad rap, and I'm sorry it does. I can hear high school me talking to friends about a girl who was dating someone older (like twenty-two, gasp) and we were all, "*Ew*, he's like *thirty*," saying the word with the same disgust one only reserves for words like *cardio* and *Caillou*.

But the truth is that being thirty is good, and my thirty-year-old-minivan-driver life is a good life. It's a life in which cracker crumbs will eternally fuse themselves into the carpet, which adds character (and texture). It screams, "Yes I *do* ignore my eyebrows completely, and no amount of Instagram tutorials can make me feel bad about it." Thirty makes the worrying-about-what-people-think clouds part and the sun shine. And I now realize I've been battling my inner-loser self my whole life, and finally I'm like, "Come here, you adorable loser. I just love you."

So now I bear-hug loser Caroline all day every day, and we are having so much fun together. It was lame of me to try to hide her away for three decades, because she brings a lot to the table—particularly an affection for yard gnomes and a very fiery monologue she's prepared in case she is ever asked her opinion of polygamist Kody Brown's hair. (Spoiler: The deep disgust prevents her from sleeping well.)

On Turning Thirty and Driving a Minivan

Obviously, the most beneficial skill I have come to completely embrace is my hand-like feet. It's my most enviable mothering quality by a long shot. For example, if I'm trying to feed the baby while the shrieking toddler needs to get into the bathroom? I open the door with my toes. Then, since the paci is on the ground and popping one more squat while holding a giant grumpy baby would cause one's legs to literally burst into flames, I pick up the paci with my toes. And don't worry—I *wash it*, because I'm not a monster . . . unless I don't have time and a tiny person is screaming at me, in which case, *look away*.

But don't worry, my thirty-year-old life is not all glamour. Recently, our eleven-month-old son ate a dead spider. He just crunched it up with his little gums and swallowed and there wasn't a thing my hands or hand-feet could do. "At least it was dead," people say, but this is little consolation. Because *he ate a spider*. "Good protein," other people say, and this is also little consolation because again, *he ate a spider*. And also, it's not like his protein needs are so extreme that we must resort to spiders. He's a baby, not a CrossFit devotee, although I will say that his fat rolls are formed into perfect little biceps, which is why he wears a lot of tank tops when he eats spiders.

So if you see me cruising around town in a slick ostrich-proof black van, ignoring my eyebrows, bumpin' my favorite audiobook, tossing Goldfish confetti-style into the backseat to Spider Eater and his sister, and driving with my hand-feet (just

37

kidding, I don't do that), don't pity me for my stereotypical subur-
banite ways. Just say, "Hey girl. How do you feel about polygamist
Kody Brown's hair?" And I will tell you: "The deep disdain has
revealed to me the profound depravity of my own soul!"

And so, friends, Romans, Town-and-Country women, do
not feel shamed by a world that does not understand the beauty
of automatic sliding doors and ages that begin with the number three. Our children may eat spiders, our floorboards may
be crunchy, and our eyebrows may need an overhaul, but there
within is the magic of adulthood: we get to like what we like and
do what works for us whether or not the world approves. This, my
friends, is exactly what our middle school selves would kill for.
We're living the dream.

7
Adelaide

Beka Rickman

Beka very much loves her husband, Ryan, even though they married before either of them realized he was a vegan. In hindsight, Beka acknowledges it might have been prudent to first research if there were any eligible bachelors within the Chick-fil-A empire. She is certain all of S. Truett Cathy's heirs have beautiful souls and smell like chicken.

I have a child who needs to be heard.

Adelaide Beth is only four years old, but she already needs direct eye contact while she's speaking, a nod of your head in acknowledgment, and responses in full sentences. If my eyes begin to wander or my replies become mumbled, her chubby little hands will cup my face and turn my head back toward her until she can look me in the eyes and ever so gently whisper, "Mommy, I don't like it when you talk to me like that."

She is completely confident in herself and expects you to be completely confident in her as well. She has an opinion, or at the very least a commentary, for every circumstance. She has a plan and a suggestion for any problem, and in her own mind believes she has complete autonomy and presidential-level veto power. She is not particularly inclined toward obedience. Why ever would she want to follow an order that is so much lamer than her own? She doesn't care if you are happy or mad at her as long as you see that she is right in the end.

It occurs to me now that I might be raising a future presidential candidate, in which case, will you hold on a sec? I need to google Georgetown Law School tuition fees . . . [*muffled scream*] . . . It appears Adelaide has a very promising future as an Applebee's manager.

No, my sweet Addy B is not one to be ignored. There is no greater offense her siblings could extend than to simply cover their ears and pretend she isn't speaking. The repercussions are immediate. And loud. And not easily placated. Have you ever considered what a meteor colliding with the earth might sound like? I have. It will sound like my four-year-old in the Target cereal aisle. And extinction is imminent.

I want to be the victim here, I really do, but my mother remembers what I did to deserve this—and she delights in reminding me. There are unverified rumors of a young me who would burst into a room filled with adult conversation and announce herself with a booming, *"Hello everyone!"* Supposedly, said child would single out those who ignored the greeting by making eye contact and reinstating, "I said, *hello."* Forgive me if I'm of the opinion that it served them right for ignoring a tiny, precious cherub. So the theatrics are apparently a genetic condition, which, when combined with my more gentle parenting style, creates the perfect environment for the development of Beka 2.0.

This morning she quietly dumped out a basket of toys and used it to climb onto the kitchen counter. Once she was up, she opened the doughnut box and ate all the frosting and sprinkles off her sister's doughnut. When I caught her red-handed, she covered her ears and ran down the hall screaming, "You are saying *nothing*, because I can't hear you."

After I addressed the tone and swept up stray sprinkles, I couldn't help but think about our similarities . . .

Have you ever tried to reach into a mirror to fix your reflection's hair or straighten her clothes, but you just keep running into yourself? If your reflection would just stay still you could set her hat on right, but instead she insists on rising up to block you. If you keep trying, you end up frustrated and a bit jolted from colliding with the mirror. And your reflection is no better off. That's what it's like for me to raise Adelaide, to be in charge of the nurture and admonition of someone so much like myself.

I see myself when I look at her, in the complexion of her skin and the flip of her hair. I'm there in the impossibly loud, the incredibly sensitive, and the ever-so-difficult challenge to correct. I see the road before her as a repeat of my own. In the years ahead, she'll put her foot in her mouth, overreact to ordinary situations, and rebel against most voices of reason. She will, at some point, begin to realize she's too loud, too prideful, or too selfish. And she'll have to acknowledge that other people can be right sometimes. She'll learn when to hold her tongue. She'll learn to listen. She'll concede her words are no less valuable even if they aren't meant for every person in her vicinity for every second of every hour of every day.

I want to warn her, to show her the last twenty years of my life so she can avoid the painful lessons. But if there's one thing I've learned it's this: we are the type who learn the hard way. And trying to force her to understand would do about as much good as painting mascara on my reflection.

So I do my best to teach her what I can, then turn my helping hands back toward myself, brush my own teeth, and button my own jacket. I will comb my own hair and straighten my skirt. Maybe then my little reflection will see and follow suit.

In spite of the energy spent corralling and correcting, I relish in celebrating Adelaide's strengths and affirming her value. I delight in her determination and in the heart she wears so boldly upon her sleeve. Her voice will be heard, and I am proud to call her my own. I choose to lift up my little reflection to Jesus, the Good Shepherd whose rod and staff have led and guided me, always with grace. The same Good Shepherd who never let me wander too far, whose discipline was never too harsh, and whose mercies are new every morning. And by His continued grace, I'll follow Him as she follows me.

8
Mommyschool

Nicole Conrad

Meet Nicole. She has complicated relationships with fictional characters. While she currently teaches a Harry Potter class for high schoolers (+), she once got a pixie cut in an attempt to look like Meg Ryan's character in You've Got Mail, *but wound up looking like the karate kid (-). There may also be Olan Mills photographic evidence of Nicole and her junior-high best friends dressed as characters from* Little Women *(+/-, it's undecided).*

As a high school English teacher, my job involves a lot of take-home work, so at any given moment I could be grading something. The same is also true of housekeeping—at any given moment I could be wiping something. Ditto for mothering. This kind of constant demand can leave me feeling guilt-ridden to the point of despair. I cannot be all things to all people. So when my daughter turned three, I decided to be some things to some people and cut back my full-time job to part-time. Thankfully, my employer agreed, and they offered me a shortened schedule. I would have fewer students, therefore less grading at home. I could spend my mornings with Claire and then pick her up from day care after her nap. As a bonus, I would get to miss lunchtime and let someone else try to get her to eat a vegetable.

Claire's day care program did circle time and learning activities after breakfast, so I was concerned that Claire would miss some educational opportunities by being home with me during that window. *I know, I know,* you're thinking, *she's three. Get over yourself. Let her be a kid.* Hindsight.

My solution was Mommyschool—a multi-media conglomerate of mommy-initiated play/learn activities from the comfort of our own home before day care drop-off. I went to the teacher supply store and got a cute calendar and bulletin board supplies to do our own circle time. I envisioned starting each day by going over the days of the week, the weather, our weekly Scripture verse, and the letter of the week. I turned one corner of my finished basement into Mommyschool central: a craft table, circle time display, homemade pennant banner, and art supplies. I began making preschool lesson plans. Each week we would focus on writing a specific letter, we would make a fun letter animal for our letter wall, we would read a book that featured the highlighted letter, and do fun crafts or science projects that tied in.

My Pinterest board was amazing. As the board developed I thought, *We'll make a ballerina bear for our letter B! We'll read*

We're Going on a Bear Hunt *and do a kinesthetic activity mirroring the movements in the book! We'll study the life cycle of a butterfly and watch YouTube videos of butterflies hatching from their chrysalides!*

Let me tell you how it really went.

"Claire, I want you to write the letter E five times on this paper like we've practiced."

"Baby, that's not an E. You know this."

"Good job on this first one, but what is this random scribble? You can do this."

"Ok, now you're just being sloppy on purpose. Let's switch to a different activity."

"How about some YouTube videos while mommy drinks her coffee?"

We read half of what felt like a zillion books. We read our Scripture verse of the week a total of five times all year. And we fought.

I remember one particularly frustrating day—she was stubborn and I was annoyed. She wasn't showing the proper amount of gratitude for all my effort. I had other things that I could be doing: laundry, schoolwork, cooking. She got sassy. I lost my temper. I'm guessing you can imagine the scenario.

So I dropped her off at day care and cried the whole way to work. I was failing at being a mom. I was sapping joy from her childhood. I was heaping condemnation and perfectionism on her and myself. The very thing I had wanted to escape by going part-time had found me—the guilt monster was at home too.

When I arrived to pick her up from day care, I still felt horrible from the anger I had expressed that morning. I knew I would need to apologize, and I couldn't stop preaching to myself about how much harder I would have to try.

I walked into the day care and saw Claire laying on her cot. She opened her eyes from her napping position, saw me, and lit up. "Mommy! I missed you!" She extended her little arms and let me lift her up and carry her to the car while she nuzzled against my neck. It was as though the morning had never happened.

This was grace. This was unconditional love. I felt God, my Father in heaven, wrapping me in His arms.

It's no surprise that this was my only year of Mommyschool. In the spring, I had my second daughter. The next year Claire went to kindergarten at the school where I teach. My Mommyschool Pinterest board has a lot of followers. And doggone it if we didn't make it through the entire alphabet. And, surprisingly, Claire is not emotionally scarred by my experiment in "quality time." That year showed me my true love for my child—that I love her not because of what she can do or accomplish, but because she's mine, and I'm hers. Her unconditional love for me showed me that my love for her was also unconditional. My try-hard self could never defeat the guilt monster that was always looming. So instead, I loosened my grip on expectations and learned what it meant to be held by the One who has freed me from mommy guilt, both now and forever.

9
Long Live the F(r)og King

Caroline Saunders

Remember Caroline? "Unforgettable!" you say, as I nod in agreement. But I actually meant to say her name was Christine, which is what her daughter's preschool teacher called her for an entire year when Caroline, a.k.a. Christine, felt too embarrassed to correct her. I'll keep my snickering to a minimum because I once had a boss who called me Kelly for way longer than a year. Solidarity, Christine.   xo, lylas, Kelly

---

The problem with preschool-aged children is that they are embarrassing. Take my two kids, for example. Whether my daughter is announcing the color of my underwear from the bathroom stall at Target, or my son is opening the stall door so that onlookers can confirm that they are indeed purple, I speak from experience that toddlers are capable of dignity destruction.

When babies are in the newborn stage, all snuggly and smelling like magic, it's hard to imagine how only a few short

49

years later they can bring dishonor on your family—like Mulan, but worse. But the truth is, these cherubs are swift and effective tools God uses to remind us we are not gloriously perfect, but rather just regular old humans who are capable of inadvertently packing moldy cheese in our kid's lunchbox. "Did you know the cheese you packed her today was moldy?" says the sweet teacher. *No, Ms. Brenda, of course I didn't. I am not a monster.*

I have left preschool red-faced many times, but location, though essential for real estate, is irrelevant for children—they do not discriminate where they inflict their trauma. When my daughter was nine months old, and I was still under the delusion that I was at least 25 percent cool, I was having dinner with some non-mother friends, and my precious baby girl pooped on every surface imaginable. All the other tables were filled with flirty college students, and I was a walking anti-glamour ad for "settling down and having a family." *Stare into your future, co-eds. There will be lots of poop.*

And then recently my not-yet-potty-trained son clogged the toilet at Swanky's Taco Shop, and I will spare you the details. I stood in the bathroom, flabbergasted, thinking, *Great. The Swanky's people are going to think this is my doing.* I could not bear this because just days before, a woman walked in on me while I was in the bathroom, and I was maxed out on embarrassment. I looked my chubby two-year-old in the eye and said, "I have met my quota. You're taking the fall for this, buddy." Then I realized that blaming him might look even worse, as though I were using my son as a cover-up for my own indiscretions, so I plotted further. We could step in the bathroom to wash our hands, and act surprised that the toilet is clogged! It was the perfect out without saying anything technically untrue, and a nonexistent stranger had to bear the shame. Oh the careful scheming mothers employ to keep their dignity intact!

But sometimes there's nothing a mother can do. My daughter has a toy she loves—a frog with a crown whom she calls, understandably, Frog King. She tends to drop her r's, so when I won't let her take the toy into church (where my husband serves as pastor, naturally), she screams "FOG KING FOG KING FOG KING," sending my soul to a dark place. "It's a frog *prince*, frog *prince*," I hiss, but you and I both know it's to no avail. It's not unusual for her to unknowingly curse the whole way into church, a scenario I mistakenly assumed would be more likely to play out in the teen years. My son doesn't curse (yet), but he does enjoy yelling, "Shake a booty!" while his pastor father cackles hysterically. Such a helpful life-partner, that one.

My husband laughs because he mostly gets to enjoy their antics inside the safety of our home, joyously tucked away from the eyes and ears of strangers. I, on the other hand, am the one who typically takes them out into the world, piling them into grocery carts, manhandling their wriggling squirming bodies into car seats, and shouting desperately to the drive thru worker, "No, I don't want any sauce! Does it sound like we are capable of managing sauce?!" or "White mocha nonfat, no whip please, oh please!" over shrieks of *Cake pop! Cake pop! Cake pop!* Oh I rue the day I introduced these savage animals to the wonders of a cake pop. I regret it almost as much as I regret introducing Costco pizza, because inevitably the slices are too overwhelming for their tiny hands, the table-to-bench distance too gaping for their tiny bodies, and the taste too delicious to miss a single bite, especially the ones that have dropped to the floor. "Man, they like that pizza," strangers comment as my children frantically eat pieces off the floor while I grab them by their ankles and wrangle them back into the cart and out of the store.

"Sticker!" they yell delightedly at the old, crusty Band-Aid plastered to the linoleum on aisle 7 at Kroger. But I won't give them the sticker because I am not the kind of mother who pries someone else's used Band-Aid off the ground just because the adorable royals command it. You may still be hearing about it on aisle 17.

My friends and I joke that moms really should get Girl Scout badges for the things we've endured. Badges such as "Defecated on in Public," and "Grocery Shopping with Demonically Flailing Child," or "Loud Accidental Obscenities." May we forge friendships on the foundation of these shared insane experiences and iron-on patches, and drink in the luxurious pleasure of taking ourselves less seriously.

So yes, we do well to buck it up and just accept that these

adorable monsters will embarrass us—profoundly. But do you know what's even better? Plotting how we will get them back when they're in middle school. I believe this to be true: Mama's day is coming, and it will be glorious.

10
Ready or Not

Catherine Chestnut

Catherine has difficulty throwing away magnets and has been involved in two separate car accidents involving the same other driver.

I'm just going to let that sink in for a minute.

"We are potty training this week," I tell the preschool teacher. She immediately assumes the I-just-got-nailed-by-a-Nerf-gun-dart look, but when I peer behind her back, no Nerf assailant is there.

"Oh," she says.

"He's in big boy underwear right now, but I can put him in a Pull-Up if you prefer."

Immediately the panicked expression fades to a hesitant smile as she says, "Only if that's okay with you . . . You see, our classroom toilet is broken, and we have to take potty field trips down the hall."

"No problem," I say, slinging my forty-ish-pound son onto the changing table. His head hangs off one end and his knees can almost bend off the other. If this training attempt doesn't work, I'm going to have to start shopping in the adult diaper section.

I turn to leave, hoping my farewell blessing to the teacher of, "He didn't have any accidents all day yesterday" would fall on optimistic ears. Plus, I handed her a freshly packed and fully stocked potty-training backpack, which included a complete change of clothes, a new pack of wipes, three pairs of underwear, three trash bags, arm-length plastic gloves, two Pull-Ups, a partridge in a pear tree, and the reversion diaper in case all potty-training hell broke loose.

Here's my strategy when it comes to potty training: when they are ready, they are ready. This comes after watching plenty of fellow trainers attempt various methods:

1. NO-UNDERWEAR BOOTCAMP: Just be sure not to schedule playdates with these people. Awkward! And it's unintentionally educational.

2. FRUIT JUICE UNTIL THE KID EXPLODES AND TURNS TO THE TOILET FOR SALVATION: Is quantity over quality really what we're going for here?

3. TYPE A MOTHER TEACHES CHILD TO BE TYPE A WITH SUCCESS CHARTING: Includes a variety of stickers of child's choice.

4. BRIBERY WITH CHOCOLATES AND OTHER SWEET TREATS
    UNTIL YOU AND THE CHILD BOTH GAIN TEN POUNDS: Don't
    worry. It's not just you. We all default to this one at some
    point or another.

Of course, all these methods have their stories of success
and failure. They can be over in a matter of days or stretch out for
months, and pretty much every method can drive mothers to the
brink of insanity.

My brilliant "wait until they're ready" method has one
major flaw: it is embarrassing.

My kids tend to be the last ones standing with diapers on.
While I am well aware that some children are "ready" at the ripe
old age of twenty months, my children haven't been deemed
ready until the approximate age of three-and-a-half. This might
have to do with the fact that I do not regard my children as ready
until they can say, in a complete and fully enunciated sentence,
"Mama, if it is a convenient time for you, I would like to use
the restroom facilities now, please." I blame their gene pool for
delayed speech development.

So, when my fourth child is in the 90th percentile for height
and weight and has the ability to dribble a ball, shoot hoops, and
drive a four-wheeler, yet is also in the 10th percentile for acquired
verbal skills, we get a rather bleak timeline for my "when they're
ready" method. I begin to think about delaying kindergarten until

he is eight while simultaneously doubting my methodology with the previous potty trainees in our household.

When the doubt has taken sufficient root, I latch on to the "chocolate til you vomit" method. *M&M's should do the trick! This child shall not be the last one in his class in diapers,* I think triumphantly.

I should have known to stop trying to force things when my son did not come home from school in the Pull-Up I put him in, but instead donned the zombie-apocalypse-quasi-wrinkled backup diaper from his backpack. After all, if peeing in a toilet conga-line style at preschool didn't inspire the kid, how were my measly chocolate offerings going to make a difference? Nevertheless, I was sure there would be setbacks, and the absence of my hovering presence surely affected his efforts at school.

The next day began with a wet Pull-Up, despite the fact that I sprinted up the stairs at the first sound of him stirring over the monitor. I helped him pick out some underwear and we went about our normal playtime and household morning activities (except that I was asking every ten minutes if he needed to use the potty). Occasionally, I made him sit on the toilet to "try" and I frequently referenced the awaiting M&Ms should our efforts succeed. And I knew he had to go—poor guy had been backed up for three days due to all the potty-training trauma.

It was lunch when tragedy struck. I started some hot dogs on the stove top, turned the heat to low, and marched upstairs to place Mr. Resistant on his ceramic throne. This time I brought the tantalizing treats with me—thinking maybe if he could actually visualize his prize, it would speed up the process. We sat together in the bathroom for a few minutes until I could smell the hot dogs on the stove. They needed to be rotated.

"Okay, let's wash your hands and put your underwear back on, buddy! We'll try again after lunch!" I headed downstairs while my sweet boy washed his hands, and I thought about adding raisins and prune juice as side dishes to our lunch. Over the audio monitor plugged into a kitchen outlet, I heard the sink water turn off, some silence, some truck noises, some Matchbox car crashes interspersed with some exclamations that sounded like "mud" and "cakes" and "look." Weird, but not unusual. I finished up the lunch prep and hollered up the stairs for him to come down for lunch.

"Mommy, cake, look!" He came running in wearing nothing but his t-shirt. My eyes narrowed to slits. I spun him around and spread his little cheeks.

"Oh crap!" I meant it literally *and* figuratively *and* spiritually *and* psychologically . . .

I sprinted up the stairs, into his bedroom, and there it was: three days worth of poop.

My son (for whom I would walk through fire) had decided that the brown loaves that landed on the carpet looked a lot like mud cakes and proceeded to run all his monster trucks through them. Deep, ground-in poo tracks zigzagged across the carpet and encrusted every Hot Wheel within a ten-foot radius. And thus is the story of how our premature potty training came to a complete and utter halt, as I'd rather custom-order size 6X Pampers than pick fossilized feces out from the hood of a Transformers Rescue Bot any day. If I must pick a potty-training poison, I choose embarrassment.

11
The Heresy of Childhood

Beka Rickman

Beka is a self-professed lover of sub-par Young Adult literature. If the plot isn't centered on teenage werewolves traveling through space to rescue a cyborg vampire princess in distress, why even read? Her book collection is vast and shameful, and her husband prefers to keep her library in the basement, so he doesn't have to look at it.

Yesterday, as I sat in the public-school carpool line, my four-year-old daughter declared in a singsong voice that she is, "all about that bass, 'bout that bass, no treble." I gripped my coffee tumbler a little tighter and took a moment to reflect upon every parenting decision I have ever made.

"Do you know any other songs you want to sing?"
"No."

I take a sip of coffee.

"May I teach you one?"

"No."

Another sip . . .

Welcome to parenting, a role in which you will be expected not only to change soiled sheets at 3:00 a.m. and wipe away ear wax with your bare finger as you walk into a public place, but also to draw lines of morality, build character, and help navigate the troubled waters of pop culture. Good luck.

Oh, and don't forget about faith. Godspeed in making sure your kids have a strong biblical foundation and well-rounded social conscience. On top of all that, they should probably eat more quinoa.

By the time I realized the pickup line had moved forward several spaces, I had inexplicably forgotten how to shift my car into drive. I waved apologetically to the cars behind me. They probably thought I was looking at Facebook on my phone again. *Not this time, haters.*

We recently moved to a new city and had to find a church, a fun experience for everyone—especially if you have three kids under the age of four. We did the sensible thing and joined the first place we visited. The childcare workers all looked well-rested and eager to be there, which is odd, but there were no pentagrams painted on the walls, nor did it smell like brimstone and goat's blood. By some miracle, it turned out to be a great community for us.

One aspect that was new to us is that school-age kids remain in the service with their parents—I believe the policy has something to do with building faith amidst tribulation. So while our oldest now sits in the service with us, she alternately uses a painting app on one of our phones and desecrates the sermon notes with unintentionally heretical drawings. Exhibit A:

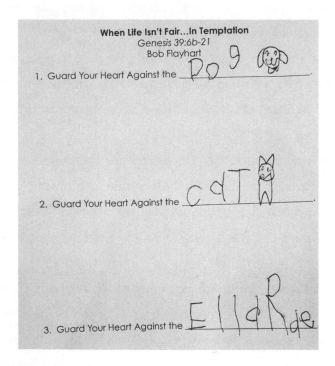

During the summer, the preschool kids join their parents in the main service as well, leaving us to wrangle a six- and four-year-old as if they are our responsibility. I know there are other kids in the sanctuary, but no one is ever as loud as your own children in a solemn environment. It's practically scientific. Every noise is amplified like submarine radar picking up torpedoes in a Tom Clancy movie adaptation. Every slap of the folding chair echoes with the ping of an incoming missile, every crayon dropped on the floor like a time bomb counting down, every whisper like the bracing before detonation.

We know firsthand what mayhem our children are capable of if we don't stay on their heels. It feels as though every eye in the room is on us . . . and those eyes are laughing . . . *wait, why are they laughing?* Oh right, because the moment our four-year-old sat down, she started a slow scan of the crowd and winked at anyone who caught her eye. Subtle, yet effective, anarchy. *Nice.*

Just when we think we've cleared all the hurdles, we find one more: the benediction song. We stand with the congregation, hearts full of faith and hope, declaring that His is the glory and dominion forever and ever, amen. On one side of me, my kindergartener embraces this time of praise with gusto (fully engaged for the first time since we denied her communion crackers as a morning snack) and boasts, "His is the gory termination foreber and eber, aaaaaahhmen." On my other side, our preschooler begins to prematurely wander toward the aisle and misinterprets the sing-a-long atmosphere as a musical free-for-all, spouting off whatever shameful pop music she overheard from my earbuds while I was power cleaning or power laundry-folding or just being generally domestically powerful. My husband and I snatch up our children like everything is on fire and haul tail before the dis in dismissed is even processed by the non-children-wrangling attendees around us. On the way out the door, we take a moment to huddle up with some fellow parents and do a quick recap of whose children were the worst-behaved and who is the most upset about it. *It's not a competition*, I try to remind them because I don't want them to be sore losers.

Up to this point I know it seems like I am upset by my children's inability to sit still and listen and be seen and not heard, but that's not entirely true. I am exasperated by it at times, but part of me is protective of it, jealous for it even. It's in those moments I watch and see that they are still naively, blissfully unaware of social expectations and traditions. They aren't giving in to peer pressure or trying to keep up with the Joneses. They aren't focused on looking their "Sunday best" and hoping everyone can see how spiritual and devout they are. They're just kids, doing their kid thing. We will teach them to stand to show respect. We will teach them to stop fidgeting because it's rude. I don't relish those milestones. Not because it isn't necessary to know appropriate social behavior, but because I don't want them to confuse what is necessary with what is important.

It never fails that my kids love to use their newly acquired church-knowledge on me at random times. The big, rapid-fire questions usually come outside of the church building while we're driving around eating gluten-saturated, white-sugar-filled donuts:

"Is God taller than the tallest building?"

"Yes."

"Could God beat up Daddy?"

"Yes."

"Does God eat?"

"Um."

"Did Jesus miss his dad when he was on the cross?"

"Yes."

"Does God love everyone the same?"

"Yes."

"Even the bad guys?"

"We're all the bad guys, baby."

The important things happen when I am utterly exhausted and bedtime curfews have been flagrantly violated. When I do not want to hear another word from anyone for the *Rest. Of. My. Life.* and a little voice whispers:

"Is God always with me?"

"Always."

"Even when it's dark?"

"Especially when it's dark."

Jesus told His disciples to let the children come to Him. I'm no historian to know how shocking and profound that was at the time, but I would wager it was—because I know how shocking it is now. Children are loud. Children are irreverent and embarrassing. They say what they are thinking and are terrible liars. Jesus knew exactly what He was doing when He welcomed them, and I want to be on board with His plan. I want the lines of truth drawn upon their hearts, not just their behaviors, even when they wrap themselves in swaddling clothes on the kitchen floor and tell me that I have to obey them because they are baby Jesus. I will mother my fidgeting, big-church-service blaspheming, pop radio fans the best I know how: from the inside out.

12
Picture Perfect

Holly Mackle

Meet Holly. She grows things, bakes things, and writes things. She is basically Martha Stewart without the insider trading.

- Abigail

I have a very prominent nose.

It's a recognizable nose, as in you can spot it at one hundred yards in profile.

Yes, it used to bother me, and yes, I kind of like it now. I don't know what is happening to me as I age, but I sure could have used a bit of this self-acceptance in the mid-nineties. (I also could have used the knowledge that a romper for school pictures is a regrettable decision, but who wants to dredge up the past.)

Let's just say I'm learning to embrace my nose.

This nose and I have a long and marred history, photographic or otherwise. I asked our wedding photographer to avoid catching me in full-on profile. If my students looked a little bored, I would catch my nose in the projector's shadow and pretend to have frightened myself. When my husband would tickle me, my common giggling retort was, "If you break it, don't expect it to come out on the other side looking the same." But nowadays, until I see myself in a photo, I kind of forget about it.

I feel fairly zeroed in on the lessons I long to teach my girls about beauty, and none of these past responses about my nose reflect them. What do I do with that? As they face the body image attacks that are certain to threaten their own self-image, how do I give them strength?

There is a photograph of my girls and me on the wall in my office. That day we were all messy-haired and still in our pjs, just filling time until Daddy got home. I decided to get out the camera because the lighting in the den was *just* so. In that moment I remember thinking, *These are just for fun because we look gross.* I, with my message of the beauty of how God sees us, almost didn't take the shot based on our appearance. I almost missed it. It hangs in my office as one of my most treasured possessions and *I almost missed it.*

How many times have I been with women I love, and when the camera comes out, so do the excuses. "Oh, I don't want to be in this one. Y'all go ahead." It's a decision usually based on temporal and external circumstances such as weight, outfit, hairstyle, you name it. They'd make comments about themselves they'd never think or say about other women. But in the end, their decision not to be photographed kept them out of the memory. Sisterfriends, when we say no to a random or spur-of-the-moment picture, what we're really saying is, "Don't remember I was here." This is far deeper than a body image issue. This is about presence, contribution, connection in friendship, and family identity. This is saying no to our heart's deep desire to be in the moment and part of the moment based on extra pounds or regrettable bangs. This is telling God that, in spite of what He says about us in the Bible, it can't possibly be true that we bear His image.

Ick.

As a woman who has put her full hope in Jesus, God looks at me and sees His son. I want to see me the way God sees me too. Covered, surrounded, sheltered, and enveloped in Christ's mighty love—that's the only frame of mind from which to decide whether or not to get in a picture.

There's another photo in my husband's office. It's of just me, in a posed school picture from a year I taught Spanish. I remember the day it showed up in my mailbox in the teacher workroom. I laughed and thought, *Why did I wear that?* And *What's with the funky thing my hair is doing?* David loved it and it's been in his office ever since. That picture is almost ten years old, and guess what? When I look at it now, all I think is, *Gosh, I look so young.*

So here's my point: sometimes giving yourself grace means getting in the picture, acknowledging your createdness, keeping your eyes on the present moment and the future memory to come . . . all while embracing the flaws. It's a good spot from which to make a decision. Jump in the picture, friends. But know, if you and I are racing to get in position, get ready for me to beat you by a nose.

13
Keep Calm and Weird On

Caroline Saunders

May I please have your attention: Caroline needs your help as she is firmly stuck in a pen name decision. Should she go with Christmas Carol? (The verrry excitable, jingle-bell-earring-wearing holiday alter ego.) Or Coach Carol? (She's the bossy gym teacher alter ego who wears a whistle and likes to make toddlers run laps.) It's a tough call . . . discuss amongst yourselves.

One of my favorite pre-motherhood pastimes was attending midnight movie premicres and feigning obsessive interest. I am *very* good at being excited, even if I'm not sure why I'm excited. Mainly, I love movie premieres because I get jazzed seeing other people's excitement as they fully embrace their current obsessions. Whether screaming at the sight of the full moon at the beginning of *Twilight: New Moon*, stretching out my hand to 3-D Justin Bieber, or spending hours perfecting my Katniss braid—all things are done in the name of hysteria participation. In a shrieking crowd united over one weird thing or another, I am a happy camper. In fact, this sums up a lot about me: around shrieking, I am a happy camper, and around camping, I am unhappily shrieking.

So yeah, I'm an advocate of the indoors, of being excitable, and of weirdness. The first is a character flaw, and I'm working on it (no I'm not), but the latter two are pretty life-giving. Especially weirdness. The best things are always a little weird, and really, when people appear too "normal," it's probably a sign that they have a giant jar of toenail clippings in their closet.

The words *Stay Weird* are boldly framed in my house as though they think they're some profound family mantra. But they *are* a family mantra. I believe in weird, I have the most fun when I accept my weirdness, and I was so pumped when my kids ended up being weird too.

For example, I'm convinced that my son, Greer, *is* Santa Claus in a toddler body. He enjoys jolliness, being round, falling down, and smelling like maple (a convenient and endearing result of his oatmeal addiction).

My daughter, Adelaide, wears accessories to bed and sleeps with five hundred stuffed animals, all named Lamb except for one, an elephant named Josephine. So we have to say, "Goodnight Lamb, Lamb, Lamb, Lamb, Lamb, Lamb, Lamb, Lamb, and Josephine." Perhaps Josephine will need to go to stuffed animal counseling one day. It's hard to be a Josephine in a bed overrun by Lambs, and in fact, it's hard to be an Adelaide in a bed overrun by Lambs. The girl is running out of room for sleeping, and it's stressing her out. "I don't know where to sit!" she cries, and I'm like, "Girl, if you'd let just half of these lambs sleep on the floor, you'd have a decent size sleeping area!" But she can't part with a single one. So we just squish those Lambs up real tight, and I say a little prayer for Josephine and a big prayer for Adelaide, this funny girl whom I love and like so very much.

A college student asked me once about parenting, and I said, "I think all kids are weird, and we need to give them space to be weird." It's just about the only thing I feel comfortable saying about parenting. In just about every other arena, I have no idea what I'm doing, but I have already seen great return in celebrating a kid's uniqueness.

I believe that weirdness has power. It makes hard tasks easier, long days shorter, and boring days more fun. I believe when we're upfront about our weirdness, our relationships are more genuine, our conversations are full of more laughter, our memories are more vivid.

Too many times I have stifled my weirdness in favor of "cool," an adjective I now believe to be both ostracizing and dangerous. Cool has never hugged us back, but weird draws us in close and gives us a noogie.

Same Here, Sisterfriend

Once when we were in Madewell (a super-cool store full of chill, fashionable clothes, and the people that belong in them), my husband Luke was playing Pokémon GO. This is a severe violation of the Madewell cool-girl vibe, and I just cannot emphasize this enough. "You cannot catch Pokémon in Madewell, Luke! This is *Madewell*," I hissed like a thirteen-year-old who can't believe her dad is wearing cargo shorts. Luke was unfazed. "I got one!" he yelled a little too loudly, though this was a welcome break from his normal "I hope this is made well" joke. Still, the midi skirts recoiled in disgust, and I felt the urge to hide behind the cognac bucket bags.

But I don't want to be that girl, the one who lets the presence of a few flannel shirts and jumpsuits and ankle boots turn her into a big fat fun-squasher. I want to be the girl who hugs back, who lets her people be themselves, who lets her husband do his little weird things, even if it's wearing camo Crocs here and there (*No, no, no, I take it back. I cannot do this*). Because "cool" is not the banner I want to wave in our house. Kids aren't born cool, they're born weird and quirky and unique, and cool is the world's attempt to snuff those things out—to make them fit into a box marked "approved."

Truly, getting to hang out with these kids makes me feel as though I'm standing under one of those big buckets at a waterpark— the ones that empty themselves out on bystanders every minute or so—sending big bucketfuls of overwhelming delight crashing onto my unsuspecting head until I'm totally drenched. (Or they make me feel like I'm drowning. It sort of depends on the day, so the metaphor holds.) They've proven to me that God's ideas are always, always the best. When I was pregnant with each baby, I was totally bewildered by how I could love someone I've never met. God planted that love deep down in my heart—a reflection of the depth of His love and goodness.

And then when I held each baby in my arms, I was still stunned: such wonder ahead! Each of their unique qualities turns my eyes into gigantic pink cartoon hearts. But truthfully, my motherly adoration for their beautiful God-given singularity is not even the best part of the story. Adelaide was already loved. Greer was already loved. Every day, this is the truest thing I know about my kids—they're already loved and celebrated. It's a done deal, forever.

The reality of being already loved by God is freedom for all of us to forever abandon the search for coolness, to know we don't need the right shoes to be marked as approved—because we already are. Psalm 139:14 in the Bible talks about how we were "fearfully and wonderfully made" in the hands of a God who is too wonderful for our minds to comprehend. It's a God whose creation proves that He thinks completely outside of the box, holds Himself to no one's standard, and begs for no one's approval. God gave giraffes black tongues, put a thousand colors in the sky, and told little sprigs of green to jut up from the earth so husbands could mow them. I think we bear God's image best when we shed our coolness and the temptation to change ourselves to suit the desires of others, and instead embrace our truest weird selves. Every bit of weirdness is a delightful gift, a reminder that God's imagination knows no bounds, and that He is a God of joyful abundance.

And that's what I want to curate in my home. Stay weird, babies.

14
My Tiny Best Friend
and Her Singing Potty

Beka Rickman

Pride and Prejudice *is one of Beka's all-time favorite books. She has spent a great deal of time categorizing and labeling the people in her life based upon their shared attributes with the five Bennet sisters. She is not so self-deluded as to believe herself to be a Jane, but aspires to be an Elizabeth. In reality she is a Kitty, desperately seeking to eschew the influence of the Lydias in her life and surround herself with wholesome and steadfast guidance. Her husband is a Mary.*

You have a baby girl. You hold her in your arms. You stare at her and your brain pops a million sparkly thought bubbles:

This baby will be my best friend.

I will cherish the bond of breastfeeding so deeply and will cry bittersweet tears when she gradually weans herself onto quinoa-and-chia-seed pudding at the age of four.

We will hold hands.

She will never bite strangers.

She will sleep in her own bed surrounded by expensive matching bedding.

I will handcraft hair bows in a plethora of pastel colors and place them just so in her delicate toddler curls. She will be so thankful and never remove them without permission.

This girl is going to have cartoon underwear and sit on a singing toilet in just two short years.

Well, some of these things came true. For the first couple of years I felt relatively on par with my hormone-induced parenting plan. Then one day . . .

I unpacked the singing plastic potty, assembled it in the living room, and my toddler and I stared at it. Then I stared at my toddler. She looked up at me with big, quizzical eyes. I faltered. *How do I teach her to go on command? Does this thing come with a dog whistle?*

"So, what you do is, um . . . You take your diaper off and you sit down and . . . "

The child was already filling the toilet bowl with apple juice and goldfish crackers. The potty sang its thanks. No, it literally sang a pre-recorded electronic jingle, "Thank you!"

I sat down on the couch to re-strategize.

When you are handed your sweet new baby, all swollen and marinated in people-cheese, you are being handed an individual.

Not just some blank slate upon which to inscribe the rules of normal human behavior, but a pre-programmed, intelligent life form full of opinions and preferences and idiosyncrasies. It is your duty to mold—nay, *herd*—your tiny being toward becoming a fully functional, capable, pants-*and*-socks-wearing adult.

"Child, if you sit here and tinkle in this thing, I will give you one chocolate chip," I began my negotiations.

"If you go potty like a big girl, you get to wear big girl panties just like Mommy!"

"The panties have Dora on them!"

"I will give you five chocolate chips."

Her initial reaction was guarded, but hopeful. She sat on the potty with her chin held high, making some appropriate grunting noises. After some determined straining, she stood up and peed down her leg. The look on her face was eager and hopeful. And in that moment I discovered something about being her mom: my desire for her to feel I was proud of her far outweighed my desire never to change another diaper. She was her own person. She would do this her own way, when she was ready. And I would be incredibly proud of her.

So for the rest of the day, I chased her around with the elaborate, bulky singing potty trying to catch the pee before it made it to the carpeted floors. I clapped and cheered every time I caught some of the dribble, and I quickly realized I was giving her a flawed impression of how this toilet business really worked.

By the end of the day, the child was wearing pee-drenched big girl panties and eating chocolate chips straight from the bag. The floor smelled strongly of vinegar. A jumbo pack of soiled Dora the Explorer panties was in the wash. I returned the proud big girl back into the diaper from whence she came and tucked her into bed. "Mommy," she said, hands on my cheeks. "Mommy, you are my best friend."

The potty training didn't really matter. Neither did the endless loads of laundry waiting for me or the chocolate chips I wouldn't be able to indulge in while catching up on the latest *Grey's Anatomy* episode. All that mattered was my park-vanquishing adventure buddy, my heart-part, my errand sidekick. She mattered. She can make mistake after mistake and I will still love her dimpled little body and expectant little soul as long as I live. In that moment, with her small hands on my face, I got the idea that she would love my dimpled body and expectant soul for a long time too. Mistakes and all.

* * * * *

P.S. A few long days turned into one short year, and the child was potty trained sometime before she turned ten. I still reward myself with chocolate chips.

Part III
Husbandfriends

Pro Tip: Avoid any suggestion, activity, habit, or theme dress that gives off the vibe "short order cook." You will be typecast.

15
On Laundry

Caroline Saunders

Caroline cannot hide her affinity for the movie Waitress, *which is about two of her favorite things: quirkiness and pie. Conversely, she cannot ever reread* The Diary of Anne Frank, *which she read far too young and which was responsible for the majority of her childhood nightmares. Caroline would now like to use this very public platform to say, "You were right, Mom."*

On any one of about a zillion different evenings after the kids are in bed, post-shower me collapses on the couch, exhausted from a long day of mom-ing. Clad in my giant fluffy robe with a yellow towel on my head, I am surrounded by a pile of laundry I heroically moved from the dryer but then, inevitably losing momentum, failed to transfer to any of the closets and drawers. Three days ago.

Laundry is a life-ruiner. It is the Groundhog Day of chores.

I am always surrounded by it, and I always complain about it. Then one dark, shame-filled day, I realized that a machine does all of the actual washing, and another one does all the actual drying. I've only got one job, and that's to put it all in the machines and then back in the closet once the real work is done, but the "putting it all back" business makes my soul shrivel up and die.

So, like any person who values the well-being of her soul, I stall (thoroughly and with great flourish) to avoid soul-shriveling things. Perhaps by eating a second dinner, creating a Pinterest board for my son's fifth birthday party (he's three), or choreographing a dance for a nonexistent show choir (which is super-cute in my gigantic robe and yellow head-towel). My husband, Luke, and I agree that the robe-towel thing is my best look, which is really saying something because I am devastatingly beautiful all the time, especially when I remember to brush my hair. Just kidding. My husband thinks the robe looks like the abominable snowman, but I think he forgets that my brain turns just about everything into a compliment and that I love snowmen. Thanks, brain!

Am I stalling? See, I'm excellent at stalling.

Eventually, all the stalling exhausts me and the laundry volume overwhelms me, so I stop choreographing and plop down in the pile and start to fold a bit. But then I get sleepy, and I take a tiny nap right there in the cozy couch-nest of clothes.

On Laundry

Eventually, laundry pile nap does the trick, and I re-emerge, invigorated and chatty. Luke, who trains himself to ignore my loud stalling methods and, coincidentally, the very quiet laundry pile, is usually sitting next to me on the couch, ever the less-obnoxious half of our duo. Except for one area: he constantly tells people that he "does his own laundry." Women at church approach me about this and congratulate me. They are in awe because I must be a very powerful woman indeed. But this confuses me because there's always a significant amount of male clothes in the piles I carry to the machines and then to the couch, and I really need to figure out which man's laundry I'm napping in.

(Update: I asked him. Luke does, in fact, believe that he does his own laundry, but his definition apparently includes grabbing a few choice items, putting them in the washer, and then forgetting about them until his wife re-washes them. I have made a mental note to share this with the women at church.)

Anyway, on at least two occasions and possibly three, I have emerged from my fluffy-robed, towel-headed laundry pile nap in order to speak with Luke and devastate him with my incomprehensible beauty, and on both occasions and possibly a third, he screamed. Screamed and literally jumped off the couch with a look of sheer terror. Because he forgot I was there. Because he thought I was laundry.

Wide-eyed Luke: "*I didn't know you were there!*"

"Of course I'm here," I say. "We were talking earlier. I just took a laundry nap."

"You look like laundry. *I thought you were laundry.*"

The first time it happened I laughed, but the second time, I cried—not because I was sad I looked like laundry, but because I was sad I *wasn't* laundry. You know, laundry gets left undisturbed for days. Doesn't that sound really good sometimes?

So now I'm jealous of the laundry pile while simultaneously looking like it, and that's kind of how things are going.

Because isn't this mothering, lunch-making, laundry-doing thing exhausting? Doesn't it often feel like we're needed everywhere by everyone but also kind of irrelevant? We want to be seen, but we want to get away. We want to melt into the laundry pile, but we also want to dominate its chaos. It's life's spin cycle, and it's confusing.

But remember that thing about my brain—the thing it does when it turns everything into a compliment? Here it is, a laundry-inspired compliment for us both:

Look at our faithfulness to provide for our families over and over again in small, unseen ways. Look how we steadfastly ensure they are clothed and fed, loved and liked. Sure, we stall, we grumble, we start to resemble the laundry pile here and there (or is it just me?), but the themes of this stage of life are faithfulness and perseverance. These words are our banner, and we carry it proudly even if no one is watching, even if our families never saw us emerge from the laundry pile. We are the steady, the silly, the safe place, the sandwich dispensers, and the sticky kiss receivers. In time, we will reap the harvest of these tiny acts of service, but for now, we will continue to fold what covers the backs of the ones we love the most and make the dinners that satisfy their bellies. It all matters because they matter, and we certainly must matter— why else would God entrust such beautiful ones to our care?

Take a nap in a pile of that truth, sisterfriend. You've earned it.

16
Sass in San Diego

Emily Dagostin

Meet Emily. She sometimes fantasizes about living in a tiny house in the backyard at the edge of her property, and she got her first smartphone in 2015.

The news came through a FaceTime call with my high school friend Brooke: she was getting hitched in six months and wanted me to be a bridesmaid for her wedding in California. I agreed on the spot, but after much squealing and rejoicing because she finally found "the one," I remembered my secret: my hunky husband and I were trying to get pregnant. We had hiked enough mountains and explored enough beaches—it was time for young love to slow its flight, settle down, and nest. I wondered what my belly might resemble in six months. A cantaloupe? A watermelon? Not wanting to hijack Brooke's exciting news, I ever-so-tactfully replied, "I'm so happy to be in your wedding, but I might be very pregnant, so I understand if that's not quite the look you're going for," because friends who have been besties since Gap overalls and awkward boob phase are free to discuss the aesthetics of pregnancy in a wedding tableau.

About a month after our call, baby Hank sprouted in my womb. This meant I'd be six months pregnant by the wedding and barely able to squeeze into my carefully-sized dress. *Thanks, Internet, for leading me to believe I would not need the maternity fit in this empire waist dress. And by thanks, I mean thanks for nothing.* As it turns out, the maternity clothing industry exists for a reason.

As the months progressed, so did my waistline (and my bustline, and my hipline, and my ankle line). Andrew faithfully dragged me to the YMCA with him four times a week, but working out just fueled the fires of my raging appetite. The inevitable was becoming obvious—I was going to be huge. I considered a full surrender: toga bridesmaid? Hawaiian-print cotton muumuu? In light of my exotic options, I decided to buck up and remind myself, *You need to try to be pretty for this trip. It's what normal people do at weddings.* But the thoughts swam in my head like sharks circling their prey. *The bride alone is six feet of tanned arms and legs. And she isn't even from California, so there's no telling what the other girls will look like. My husband will forget I exist! This is the start of the rest of your sorry mom-body life! It's all stretch marks and gravity from here on out.* So, feeling like a tiny fish at the bottom of the ocean, I had some serious camouflaging to do—wardrobe prepping, eyebrow plucking, and booby boosting—especially since Victoria's Secret wasn't doing so hot at keeping my secrets anymore.

When Brooke's big day came, the sun granted her request for a stunning and bright background, dotted with us, her very best friends—the toasted, roasted bridal party, ablaze with support for this matrimony, and beginning to sweat under magnanimous solar rays. Squinting, I pasted on a glistening smile and stood tall and straight, knockers up to make my Mimi proud, and nearly passed out during the closing prayer. Oh that blasted sash! *Plus* the cinching belt was squeezing all-that-is-not-holy on my hips into the ornamental bodice I was wearing. I had closed my eyes and imagined myself a goddess of fertility leaning leisurely onto one of the stately columns crowning a lush veranda. I thought my closed eyes would exude holiness, but apparently the commoners below me detected "medical emergency." A young female guest told me afterward she considered racing up the aisle to catch me as I was clearly about to pass out. So much for my goddess aura. That dress was literally a shimmery second skin, so I peeled it off when the contractions started. *Relax,* I told myself, *this is not labor—*just extreme thirst and exhaustion and sweating-out-of-every-orifice kind of contractions.

Two Gatorades later, my husband (who that night resembled a young James Bond) escorted me into the reception. His hand on the small of my back sent a little tingle down my spine, making me feel nineteen again. Lights floated over the dance floor like fireflies. Rows of white tablecloths arrayed with succulents and lilies surrounded us. Men wore tuxedos, and the women were resplendent in classy floor-length gowns—truly enchanting. My keen pregnancy nostrils registered something of the strongest appeal considering my current situation: wine. A red, velvety, Southern California merlot calling to my olfactory nerve like Fred Segal to a Kardashian. There's no preparing a pregnant sniffer for that. So after I stuffed my face with prime rib, save one bite ("That's my girl," said my husband), I quietly asked the waiter for exactly one ounce of red wine. And I plunged into sensory overload with each tiny, luscious sip.

Dinner gave way to dancing and the classy scene took a crazy turn when the glow sticks came out. I was surprised at my agility on the dance floor—barefoot, of course. My husband and I stormed the floor to "Superstition" since nobody gets me moving like Stevie Wonder. So there I was with melting makeup and wind-tossed hair, surrounded by twirling lights and light-hearted celebrants, barefoot and comfortable in a newly-donned cotton maternity dress (no more sequin sausage casing for me, thank you), fully embracing my ever changing mom-bod, and feeling uninhibited by the safe embrace of my husband and the sultry sounds of Stevie. I saw the joy of the moment in Andrew's smile and in the gleam in his eye. I was sweetly reminded not only that *I've still got it* but that I was his and he was mine.

I needed that moment, dancing with the man I love. It reminded me that, in spite of the tortuous bridesmaid bodice and edema-stricken ankles, I was still me. Motherhood might have temporarily thwarted my enjoyment of celebratory tipsiness and my ability to tolerate long stints in heels, but it hadn't killed my groove or that sparkle in Andrew's gaze. And now, home in Alabama, back in the day-to-day of marriage and motherhood, I look back on that memory with gratitude. All that superstition about the mothering days? The whispers that the good days have passed? That "ain't the way," as Stevie would say. And it took a pregnant dance in wine country to remind me that no matter how much my life and body have changed, no matter how many little people are currently whining for a juice box, I can still bring the sass. And that's something to take back to Alabama to keep them home fires burning.

17
The WAFFLE League

Holly Mackle

Holly has the most twinkly eyes when she is excited and starts fanning her armpits when she is nervous, a sure sign that she watched far too much SNL as a preteen.
- Catherine

It's going to take a minute to get where I'm going. You might want to pack a snack.

I think the only appropriate place to start is to say that I am a happily married woman. However, as you might recall from your school days, there is an exception to every rule: during fantasy football season, I am simply a *married* woman.

For lo, though my husband be handsome and wise, he is into *all* the football. I understand that many husbands (and some wives) follow teams, even large swaths of teams known as conferences, or even individual players they feel a certain connection to. My husband feels connected to football—all the football. And the players—all the players. Because when you play fantasy foot-ball, all aspects of football are relevant. Everyone you've drafted to your team is either active that week or benched, so you have to figure out if you made a good call playing Mr. So-and-So or if you accidentally left your star on the sidelines. Keep in mind, all of this is purely hypothetical: even though a player wasn't *actually* on the bench—meaning he really played in his real-life game—he's still metaphorically benched to you, and you're lauding or heckling yourself at whether or not you made the right call. This statisti-cal information is also pertinent for every other league member's team, giving no end to the relevance of what *many* would deem deeply irrelevant information.

Listen, if I were to create a metaphorical bench, it certainly wouldn't look like a sweaty, smelly, athlete's-foot-infected bleacher bench. It would be cute and upholstered in supple (my husband David hates that word, so I just had to work it in) fabric and tacked with those gorgeous deep brass nail heads. And it would have a delightfully colorful Kantha throw lazily draped over it in a way that says, "Yeah, I just kinda tossed it there and it landed like that." Not entirely unlike the effortlessly messy hairdo of the cute frat guy in college who was unencumbered by life and way out of my metaphorical league—the one who would show up at 8 a.m. Pre-cal with tousled hair and the *Yeah, I just woke up like this* expression. I ended up spending 40 percent of class wondering if he had actually woken up before I had and tried really hard to get his hair to do that supremely hot hotness messy thing to distract me from cosigns and parabolas and tangents and, oh look, how did I get here . . . *happily married . . . fantasy football.*

You see, in fantasy football, everyone you didn't draft is also crucially important, because they were either drafted by your opponents or they're exceeding ESPN's projections—or they're about to be one of the two. This means that you have to know if they are playing or benched so you'll know who to pull for and against, which makes all of the players on all of the teams on all of the days totally relevant to your life. Some of you are nodding, and to you I say, "Let's be friends," and to the rest of you (the confused ones) I say, "Does my bareMinerals cover my thinly veiled jealousy?"

For years, David has espoused the theory that all of our marital discord would be righted if only I could get into *all* the football. He'd probably even be mollified if I could just get into a *little* bit of football. Let's not have any discussion as to whether or not I have tried. When we are invited to a football thing at a real live stadium, David goes for the football and the ambience and the team solidarity; I go for the catering. When we are invited to a friend's house to "watch the game," David goes for the high fives and the overly-enthusiastic whooping and the buffalo dip, and I go hoping the hostess really isn't into the football either and wants to chat for four hours about absolutely anything else.

Can we stop here? Did you catch that? *Four hours.* Is anyone but me aware of this little-recognized fact that one football game lasts *four* hours? I've played less painful Monopoly games. Risk, anyone?

Yes, of course I understand this is a competitive thing within the league. I get it. And David has won the whole thing in his league. He wants to make sure I say that. And I can see his face nodding with that mischievous grin on it right now like, "Right? C'mon! High five?!" And David, if you've made it this far in this specific piece, you should probably recognize the high probability that most readers are not cheering for you right this second.

Considering the way the NFL as a corporation seems to be taking its cues from Disney's marketing department, I'm convinced football is trying to take over our lives. You see, the pro games are no longer on one predictable day. Oh no, it's not just Sunday afternoon anymore! It's Sunday night, Monday night, Thursday night, and Sunday morning because they're taking teams over to play in London to try and make fans out of the Brits. *Hey, Roger Goodell, would you leave Mr. Darcy out of this? You've gone too far!* I want to dispatch carrier pigeons with rolled-up notes or use my best Mary Poppins impression at the very least to say: "They're trying to trick you! It's not the same football!"

In case this is wordy or unclear, or in case any of you feel the need to post a warning in your house for this specific purpose, allow me to offer you this easy-to-read-and-interpret diagram:

But I haven't even told you why I'm writing this deeply important and incredibly thoughtful think piece yet. And I do have a point, really, I do. Actually, it's less of a point and more of an invitation. Ladies—*sisters*, if you will—I would like to cordially invite you to join my very exclusive league. The meetings are rare (if ever), there are no dues, and the requirements are scarce . . . but I dare you to find a more committed and devoted group of women. We are bound by angst, tears, necessity, commonality of suffering, and a deep disdain for imaginary, time-consuming sports. Please consider this your formal invitation to join:

The WAFFLE League
for
Women Against Fantasy Football Leagues Everywhere

Let me know what size shirt you want. They're going to be super cute.

18
The Talk

Abigail Avery

Abigail's husband, Jason, believes she is a terrible driver. This is entirely untrue. She is efficient. He also falsely believes she reads more people.com and TMZ than he does.

I always thought I'd be a mom to lots of boys. Boys are physical, not emotional. Boys get over things: forgive, forget, move on, avoid drama. They are also loud. And break things. They fight, smell, sweat, and hygiene is, well, often a mere suggestion. These are my people. This is the familiar rubric from which I hoped to parent because, quite frankly, I am terrified of girl maintenance. All the moods, the long talks, the tears, and the drama. My element is more a shoot-me-straight and tell-me-like-it-is boutique, a rough and tumble environment, probably attributed to growing up with older brothers and no sisters. So I envisioned a home with my husband, full of messy boys who drank milk like water, ate as much pasta and dessert as I could supply, and hung out in a living room that some might mistake for a Play It Again Sports. It was a dream with babies in Jon Jons, little boys with patchwork plaid bedding, and teenagers in khakis and golf shirts. And I was the thriving wife and mama, secretly happy I escaped hair bows and ballet recitals.

In 2007 I found myself pregnant with our first child, entirely convinced it was a boy. I remained confident through the duration of the pregnancy, choosing mahogany furniture and a nice neutral blue for the nursery. No pink in sight. That December, we welcomed our precious baby into the world.

A daughter.

She was healthy and beautiful, but she wasn't a boy. So, thankful as I was, I had to adjust my dream to include at least one girl. Slowly, I began to accept pink and decided I could enjoy this after all. I dusted off my sewing machine and learned to smock. *Girls are great*, I told myself. And I believed it, burying that dream of all boys.

Until I found out I was pregnant again.

Somewhere between the morning sickness and diaper changes, the floodgates of desiring a son re-opened. I tried to hold them back, placing sandbags around my heart. I was older. Wiser. Full of gratitude for the healthy baby we had and loved. I told myself (and anyone who asked), that I didn't care if this next baby was a boy or a girl. That's what I said out loud. But inside, I desperately wanted a boy. We opted not to find out the gender during that pregnancy and it wasn't out of anything but self-preservation—I was afraid of disappointment.

Two days after my due date, our son was born. He was healthy with the loudest lungs I've heard on a newborn to date. We were elated.

A short nineteen months later, we found ourselves back in the delivery room. A surprise pregnancy, followed by another surprise: a second baby girl. With three children under four, I fully abandoned dreaming about a home full of boys, in the hopes that we all just lived through the day. It took us a while to hit a stride (or even take a baby step) during the next two years, but eventually we settled into a rhythm of sorts—also known as online shopping, frozen meals, paper plates, and yoga pants. My husband Jason was right along for the ride, helping as much as his work schedule allowed. He loved the girls and had a strong affection for the boy too, which, if you ask me, took him by surprise. He felt a duty to teach the boy about all things boy—especially since he was surrounded by girls for a large part of the day. He often told the boy about various sports, trying to interest him in any kind of ball, and of course potty training him outside. Ninety-nine percent of these father-son bonding moments were fun to watch and experience. There came a time, however, when I made Jason promise that he would have "the talk" with the boy.

The Talk

Most dads probably dread "the talk." At three years old, I felt it was time. And Jason agreed. The boy was more aware of his body and its functions. Jason had to take a firm yet compassionate approach to instill a sense of responsibility about the subject. We considered waiting until he was older, but the risk was too great. *What if someone teaches him about it at preschool?* we wondered. No, we needed to get out ahead on this one.

So, intentionally and by design, at the tender age of three, Jason sat the boy down to instill in him one of life's most important and valuable lessons: *You may never, ever, under any circumstances, no not ever . . . catch a fart and throw it in a girl's mouth.*

Let's just let that sit for a moment.

And maybe just one more.

Have you sufficiently recovered? Good.

It might seem an odd request to make of your child. I'm sure a large portion of the general population would even question, "Is that a thing? I didn't know that was a thing." If knowledge of this practice has evaded you thus far, do not feel alone. I, too, was once ignorant of these ways. But, be ignorant no more! Gas-throwing is a practice handed down from older boys to younger, on sports teams, in locker rooms, on playgrounds, and even in discipleship groups. Let me explain: The practice involves the perpetrator reaching a hand around his own southern cheeks in a cuplike manner as he feels the need to pass gas. Once the gas is released, the hand is closed quickly around the air, much like catching a cricket, or lightning bug. Next, in this catch and release sport, the perpetrator throws the now-captured contaminated air into a target's face as quickly as possible before it dissipates, which would render the weapon entirely worthless. I have been told that boys of all ages (and a few unsuspecting lock-in parent chaperones) have fallen victim to this insidious prank. And I must admit that I too have suffered from the hurling of flatulence.

It was the summer of 2003. Jason and I had been married for less than three months and were tracking right alongside Nick Lachey and Jessica Simpson settling in as newlyweds. We were weeks away from starting graduate school together, and married life still felt a bit like playing house. Each day was a learning opportunity: how long we brushed our teeth, our alarm sound preference, snooze habits, etc. I was also testing my skills at consistent meal preparation. One particular evening, after slaving over jarred spaghetti sauce and boxed pasta, we decided to take in some forgettable reality television from the comfort of our bed. Excited to use all our new wedding gifts, I had recently ironed our monogrammed duvet cover and it was ever-so-satisfying to settle in and enjoy the freshly made bed. I'm not entirely sure where things went wrong. I do know I was completely blindsided. At some point, probably during a commercial break, the idea must have struck Jason. Perhaps he had been lying in wait, patiently plotting for the intersection of need and opportunity to perpetrate this prank, or maybe the onions in the spaghetti sauce sparked his

The Talk

spontaneity. Regardless of premeditation, Jason rolled over onto his side, seemingly to grab a drink of water, but instead cupped his southern cheeks. At that exact moment, a scene of hysterical nature appeared on the television screen, causing me to guffaw with laughter, leaving my mouth wide open. As Jason expertly encapsulated the polluted air, he raised his arm to throw it at my face as quickly as possible, neglecting to look toward his target for fear of losing his air bomb. His failure to aim resulted in his hand opening directly over my gaping mouth and forcing the infected air inside. The only delicate way to describe what happened next is that I ate his fart.

At first, I had no idea what had just happened. What did I taste? What did I smell? I began to gag immediately. Jason began to laugh. As my gagging increased, his laughter compounded, rendering both of us unable to speak—I was unable to ask, "What in the world was that?" and he was paralyzed from explaining his dastardly deed. I continued gagging, he continued laughing. The gagging increased so much that I began to cough violently. Unable to shake the smell or taste of what I had just inhaled and ingested, I vomited spaghetti all over the brand-new, freshly pressed and expertly monogrammed duvet, our bed, and the carpet in our apartment. There I sat, a wife of less than twelve weeks, in a puddle of my own gas-eating-induced vomit, having no idea what WMD had just been released on me. At some point during my heaving, Jason began to hyperventilate with laughter. Due to his pervasive silent howling, he began to turn the slightest shade of blue from decreased oxygen. He was so overcome with hilarity that he was entirely unable to assist me in any way as I began to clean up. So, I picked up regurgitated noodles and unloaded an entire bottle of Resolve, worrying about our security deposit.

Miraculously, about the time cleanup was complete, he regained his composure and explained what had happened. I sat, dumbfounded. "Who does that?" I asked. *"Who does that,"* I repeated. I thought growing up with brothers had illuminated me to the ways of the male species and their pranks. Tickle someone until they pee on themselves? Sure. Belch the alphabet? Let's time it. Clothesline your brother as he passes you in the kitchen? All day. But throwing a fart? I had never . . . So, I asked for a recitation of the origin of this prank. Who taught him? How widespread is it? Do other men do this? Had he ever been a victim of it? Does the Health Department know this goes on? Does it transmit disease? He explained what he could, but nothing could mediate my initial shock. Then, Jason made his first and most serious marital promise since taking our vows. He promised to *never*, under any circumstances, release that torture on me, or any other female, ever again.

Horrified by my newlywed experience, I shared the story with a few close female friends. They too seemed utterly shocked and disgusted. None had heard of this prank, and they were all appalled. Jason also shared the story with some of his friends, who immediately reacted with disbelief. Unlike my female supporters, their dismay was not of the practice itself (they were well-versed in this secret knowledge), but that Jason's weapon was so potent it induced vomiting. Once I corroborated his story, the phone calls to him started pouring in and the high fives and congratulatory hugs began. They might as well have bought cigars and opened a bottle of bourbon. I began to wonder how it was possible that such a clandestine hoax had almost completely evaded me and most other women. I thought I knew so much about my husband. We dated for two years before marriage and went through what seemed like extensive premarital counseling. We had plans for how to attack finances, divide housework, and ensure date nights, but no one had ever mentioned what to do when your husband serves you his spoiled, expelled air. Looking back, it was really just the first introduction into a number of topics I did not know (or was simply too naïve) to anticipate in marriage.

Fast-forward ten years to when Jason and I were faced with bringing up our own son, the boy I had hoped and longed for. As Jason prepared for "the talk," he knew it was of paramount importance to train the boy beyond mere technique, and instead focus the majority of his time on proper target acquisition. Perhaps they would take a trip to the park and observe viable options, or find a safe friend to help in discerning appropriate victims. Either way, the message had to resonate that girls, women, the elderly, and anyone with asthmatic tendencies must be protected at all costs.

Jason dutifully reported back that the conversation went well. The boy was receptive, teachable, seemed to comprehend and has thus far followed the established parameters. But, the boy is still young, and middle school still lies in wait. It's a subject we will revisit repeatedly in order to cement the teaching.

As for now, fourteen years have passed since that fateful evening with my husband and I am happy to report that he has honorably kept his promise to resist this very specific temptation. As I reflect on my one-time dream for a house full of boys, I wonder if we would have had the stamina to properly train all those boys in the etiquette of man-pranks. There are plenty of challenges with girls as well, but I am more thankful for all things hair bows and princess now, and I have increased respect for families of boys. And because I know there are countless families raising boys along with us, I want to invite parents across the land to follow our lead on what might seem to be an obscure issue. Please do not underestimate the importance of this topic. Please, talk to your sons and talk to them early. If you don't, their friends will, and our daughters and their daughters after them will suffer. The future of our girls rests in your hands.

19
Trudy

Beka Rickman

When Beka was fourteen, she fell off the horse she was standing on and broke her back. She does not regret standing on the horse, only falling off.

---

[1]These six things the car owner doth hate; yea seven that are an abomination to him

> [a]a cracked windshield,
>
> a missing rim,
>
> and a slipping transmission;
>
> [b]a cooling system that deviseth never to hold coolant;
>
> a tachometer that oscillates when idling;
>
> [c]a cracked motor mount, and a car that soweth discord amidst a marriage.

Okay, okay, so the Bible doesn't actually reference car problems as an abomination. (I checked.) But those of you in the Clunker Club know it should.

We've been card-carrying club members since my husband was in engineering school, when my in-laws gave us their hand-me-down car. She was what the manufacturer referred to as a "value package." No leather seats, no key fob or navigation system, no auxiliary cord or heated seats. She did come equipped with a cassette player and manual window cranks. She was reliable and had high safety ratings, and to me she was heaven on wheels. I named her Trudy.

Trudy may not have had the flashiest pair of headlights on the interstate, but she was free, and she was all mine. In a season of our marriage when my husband Ryan was a full-time student and part-time employee, and I was home with two very small children, Trudy was a dream come true. We didn't have much, but we had a good car. My children were on Medicaid, but I didn't have a car payment. My pantry was filled primarily with Great Value brand mac and cheese, but there were no auto repair bills.

By the time Ryan graduated, Trudy had faithfully carted us to countless doctor's offices, parks, libraries, and grocery stores. We'd sailed past the 200,000-mile mark on the odometer without even blinking. And when Ryan's hard work finally paid off and he accepted a job as an engineer, Trudy took us across the state to start a new life. I could practically hear her purring with excitement, but in my enthusiasm, I might have heard purring rather than the cracking of the motor mount.

All our dreams of good school ratings and savings accounts were coming true, but they were coming true a hundred miles from what we knew as home. A hundred miles from our friends and family. A hundred miles from free babysitting! We were finally able to pay our bills, but we were completely alone. We needed a date night. We needed camaraderie. Trudy, now donning mismatched headlights and dull silver paint, was once again our beacon of hope in the darkness. We strapped our little people in their car seats, handed them baggies of Goldfish crackers, and retreated north to go "home" for the weekend. And then we went back the next weekend. And again the next. And the next . . .

We rolled down the windows when the air conditioning went out. We sang songs with our kids at the top of our lungs. We ate so much fast food that the door handles and window cranks glistened with grease, and the fabric seats held the tangy scent of honey mustard. The girls would get lost in a game of "I Spy" while Ryan and I held hands over the console, rehashing our week and dreaming about the future. When our third child was born, Trudy carried him home in his infant seat, snug between his sisters while the gentle rattle of the engine lulled him to sleep.

Somewhere around the 250,000-mile mark, the long road trips became more infrequent. The kids had birthday parties and gymnastics, plus our church and Sunday school classes kept us busy. Finally, Trudy was beginning to fall apart at the gaskets—literally. The clanking starts and sputtering stalls were becoming embarrassing, and the roadside SOS calls were problematic.

But my mechanical engineer husband wasn't going to let her go without a fight. We found YouTube videos and DIY blogs to help keep her going. I often heard him tinkering away in the garage after dinner, sometimes late into the night. The occasional phantom profanity would echo up through the vents as I slept alone in our bed. We even ordered cheap parts from China. When they arrived, Ryan would spend hours taking the engine apart and putting it back together. Within a few months those parts would begin to warp or crack and we'd be back at square one, so we wised up and ordered parts directly through the manufacturer (also in China). Ryan continued spending weekends as a grease monkey, but as soon as one problem got solved, another would pop up. For all the good Trudy had done us, she was becoming the third wheel our marriage didn't need. We knew our time with Trudy wouldn't last much longer.

As we sat on the side of the road watching smoke billow from her hood for what I knew would be the last time, sweat began to drip from my brow and I, without hesitation, grabbed my phone and called a friend to pick up my kids from the scene. Ryan was already on his way with more coolant, and they both arrived at the same time. We laughed at the absurdity of it all as my friend handed us bottles of cold water. It was then I realized we weren't

Trudy

alone anymore. We had bought our first home, our kids were in great schools, and we had friends we could both trust and rely on. Trudy had seen us through. She was never the prettiest on the lot, but she was the car we needed to take us where we were going. She was the bridge that spanned between our lives in two different cities, and the crutch we needed as we grew into a new season in life. And now we were finally ready to say goodbye.

So here's to you, Trudy, for always getting us where we needed to go. I might own a newer car with fewer miles and more amenities, but I'll never own a better one.

20
The 80/120 Principle

Cara Johnson

Meet Cara. She spends October through May with icy feet but will never ever ever give up her nightly bowl of Publix Chocolate Cookie Quarry frozen yogurt, even when it means she has to sleep with her electric blanket on all night to recalibrate her body temperature.

"If it's okay with you, I'm going to cut the grass now," my husband, Phil, said. "It'll take about an hour." Throughout twelve years of marriage, cutting the grass has been part of his job description, right between "getting into a cold body of water with our kids" and "putting together IKEA furniture."

This time when he says, "It'll take an hour," I translate: *I must now entertain kids alone for one hour on a Saturday.* It was one of the first shorts-and-t-shirt days of spring, so I fought their inertia and began to shoe and shoo them outside. Fifteen minutes later, after they'd gone potty for the second time and located their shoes and changed their minds about which shoes they wanted to wear, then flailed on the floor that the shoes weren't tight enough and asked for different shoes for their next birthday that wasn't for another seven months . . . we finally made it outside. I'd successfully waddled down to our garage with a baby on one hip and two sippy cups, snacks, and phone in the other hand.

"I know! Let's move the cars out and ride bikes in the garage and driveway!" It was a pat-yourself-on-the-back moment for me. I even let the kids take turns sitting in my lap at the wheel as I backed out the cars. With a bright blue helmet on one little head and a bright pink one on the other, they started pedaling while the hip-baby and I rearranged all the stuff I'd brought with me, which I now realized qualified us for a TLC show on doomsday preppers.

Fast-forward now through a haze of bike accidents and Band-Aids, one-handed disciplining, nursing while helping the three-year-old steer her bike, and trying to solve the afternoon's greatest problem: who would get to push the pretend lawn mower behind Daddy? I still maintain that, despite what my husband's stopwatch said (because he's the kind of guy who times himself to see how fast he can mow), it had been longer than fifty-eight minutes. I was sure of it.

As I stood at the top of our yard looking down at him push this machine back and forth—a machine that blocked out all other noise and increased his heart rate for an hour, I thought: *Why am I not doing that? It's a free hour of exercise, productivity, and alone time when the kids know they can't ask me for anything because I literally won't hear them. It's brilliant!*

I waited until after dinner and the rhythmic rise and fall of the kids' freshly-bathed chests before opening my mouth about the mowing situation. (Because now that I wanted his job, it was a *situation*.)

"So, you know how you always do the mowing? I think it needs to be my job." It was best not to mince words about things of such importance. After Phil patiently listened to my list of reasons, his only request was that he still do the smaller front yard and edging while I did the larger back yard. A little peculiar, I thought, but maybe he wasn't quite ready to let go of a job he sort of liked all these years.

Then I remembered our 80/120 Principle of marriage.

Perhaps you're not familiar with it. Since it could be instructive and, dare I say, *revolutionary* to your own marriage, I'll share some of the inner workings of mine. The 80/120 Principle states that one of us (ahem, me in this scenario) works with the efficiency of twelve Roombas but will only get 80 percent of a job done. In the end, it will be done quickly and look significantly, noticeably better, but it will not by any stretch be perfect. The other one of us (cue husband) will do every job to absolute, deliberate perfection. It will take approximately four hours, but you could lick syrup off your bathroom floor with complete assurance that you won't need the attention of an infectious disease specialist.

Not that syrup is ever on my bathroom floor (and definitely not last Wednesday).

The 80/120 Principle used to be a source of contention in the early years of our marriage. Phil would go behind me when I cleaned the kitchen and I'd quip "you're not *done* yet?" when he was washing his car or folding laundry. But then one day it occurred to us that our 80/120 deal was one of our best assets as a team. It made us a power couple—we just had to learn to play to our strengths. Need your house to look like you spent the day cleaning, but you only have fifteen minutes? I'm your gal. Want your bathroom corners pee- and cracker-crumb free? Phil's on point.

After Phil requested that the front yard continue to be his job, I realized he didn't want to keep it because he loved mowing—he wanted to keep it because he knew he'd make it look better. Mow the corners at exactly ninety degrees. Edge in ruler-straight lines. Mow some geometrical equation into the grass itself so that every time he came home he could sit back and sigh and think to himself, *Well done, Phil. Well done. If this career built on blood, sweat, and multiple years of graduate studies doesn't work out, I think you've got another good future, kid.* And he was right. He *would* make it look better. And it mattered to him, so I gave him that one. In return, he gave me forty-five minutes of uninterrupted time to do something energetic and progress-oriented that did not happen at a gym. Fair enough.

A week later, the grass and weeds and clover and wild onions that are in my back yard had raised their blades and shoots up in the air as if to say, "Me! Me! Mow me!" It was time to come through on my part of the mowing. The last time I'd mowed was in early high school when I rocked the wispy bangs and there was no such thing as a self-propelled push mower. It was a lot like driving with no power steering, and resulted in blisters between my thumb and index finger as well as anxiety that I'd mow over hornets and be stung two hundred seventeen times. I also had to ask my brothers to pull the starter rope for me—something I didn't want to repeat this time because I didn't want no help from nobody.

Pumping his legs in the swing, my oldest asked, "Mommy, why do girls *and* boys mow the grass instead of just boys?" I could feel every feminist message I'd ever clung to clawing up my throat. I closed my eyes, inhaled deeply, exhaled audibly, and smiled. "Because, mowing the grass isn't a boy thing *or* a girl thing. It's just something people do. Sometimes boys like to do it and sometimes girls like to do it, and in our family Mommy and Daddy *both* like to do it, so we take turns mowing different parts of the grass." Close enough.

Phil pushed the mower from the garage to the top of our backyard hill and gave me a few general instructions: go clockwise; if it sounds like it's getting clogged, lean the mower back and let the blades spin for a few seconds; squeeze the bar while cranking it up. He then walked away, leaving me to conquer the backyard. Behind my game face was a heart of helium; behind his nonchalance was a tongue bitten more times than I'll ever know.

Despite what would be many shortcomings, I started that sucker all by myself, *thank you very much*, and began pushing fast enough to get my heart rate up so it would count as a workout. My kids pumped their legs on the backyard swings as Phil simultaneously entertained them and smiled his smile that told me he was trying to be chill but also watching me like a hawk. Was he happy for me or masking criticism? Both, I decided, and kept pushing. I tried to avoid eye contact with the kids, who were quickly off the swings and making ornate sign language gestures trying to tell me something that their father three feet away could and would help them with. The kids eventually gave up trying to communicate with me and decided to head back inside to cool off.

I was following instructions and making progress quite nicely, taming my mutt of a backyard into something more respectable. Unlike cleaning inside, where little people crush crackers at the exact spot I swept approximately four seconds before, mowing the outside would look good for an entire week before those grassy little sprouts grew tall again. And knowing that a completed task of mine would last for more than four seconds stretched my face into a smile right there in the middle of the job.

Between the earthy smell of freshly cut grass, my salty upper lip, muscles taut from effort, and the mix of blood and adrenaline coursing through my veins—I could have mowed for hours. Every few minutes, I'd look at the set of windows lining the back of the house and see Big Brother Phil looking down on me. Was that disapproval I sensed in his eyes? Entertainment? Pity? Didn't matter. I was doing it, wasn't I?

An hour later, my shoes rimmed with green, I was finished. I'd given the yard a mighty handsome haircut. Within minutes, Phil came out, and I couldn't help remembering the childhood days of Dad checking my math homework. Sweet Phil started with a strong, "The yard looks great!" But as I answered, "I know I didn't do everything right, but man it felt good," I could see in his eyes that he wanted to say more, so I decided to make the pointers a game. "Okay, let me see if I can guess how many things I did wrong, and you tell me if I missed any." He was in. Apparently, I knew my weaknesses well, listing things such as, "I 'vacuumed' certain sections," "I went over the same spot about four times," and "I missed some corners."

"You literally *cut* corners," he said with a grin.

"What else did you expect from the 80 percent?"

"True. And the good thing is, it's just the backyard."

"*Just* the backyard?"

We bantered like the old lovers that we are, but there it was—the truth: I'm a backyard mower. And he's absolutely right. And I'm absolutely okay with it.

Because in the end, our yard looked good—really good. The front was manicured, the back was tamed. I'd voiced my need to conquer and produce something I could see, and Phil had let go of making our backyard resemble a golf course. But the thing is, no matter how perfectly we play to each other's strengths and power-team the heck out of life, the grass blades keep raising up their little arms—needy little things. And our kids keep needing their shoes tightened and found and replaced and changed. And I keep trying to feel good about myself by doing something new or better or different. And there is nothing new under the sun.

Moments after Phil and I had dissected my mowing skills, my middle little ran up to me, grasped my hand in hers, and said, "Mommy, you did a great job!"—words I'd never once heard for sweeping crumbs off the floor.

Part IV
Kidfriends

Pro Tip: No matter what "they" say
(because toy manufacturers will say anything to make a
dollar), never ever purchase a toy mermaid that
cannot be submerged in water.

21
For Olivia, My Third Child

Holly Mackle

Holly has a remarkable knack for enthusiasm. She's the only person I know capable of expressing genuine Christmas-morning excitement over a meal of beans and rice.
- Pamela

Dear Olivia,

I'm sorry I can't remember if your middle name is Elizabeth or Catherine.

I'm sorry I ignore you.

Forgive me that I think you are a source of constant frustration—by being fought over, thrown in irritation, and carried, packed, stuffed, clutched, or buckled wherever we go.

My bad for allowing Ellie to think you are a real American Girl doll when you actually cost seven hundred dollars less than a real American Girl doll. It's not that I've perpetuated the tale; I've just never exactly corrected it. Thank you for playing along.

Apologies for the dramatic haircut. I now realize Ellie may be a bit too young for unsupervised chewing gum. That's on me. Have I told you how good you look with a bob?

Also, I'm sorry you got that snake bite in your eye and had to be in the hospital for six days. I hope the *Paw Patrol* Band-Aids helped.

And about Ellie's imagination . . . it's genetic.

I'm sorry I steer the Costco buggy away from the aisle that holds your accessorized pony box set, complete with a saddle just your size. If you'd like to get into riding, you should talk to Mimi.

Can we keep it between us that I don't even buckle your seatbelt when Ellie asks me to?

I'm sorry I neglected your education that time she told me to homeschool you while she was at real school. I know you remember that all I did was park you on the floor with a piece of paper and a crayon. Thanks for covering for me when she got home. Appearance is everything.

I assure you I have the deepest distress over the grandiose declarations Ellie makes about your preferences, likes, and dislikes. I'm sure she is wrong about most of them, namely your penchant for wearing a fur muff in ninety-four-degree weather and how you *have* to sleep with your arms outside the blanket when it's freezing cold. We're still working on our understanding of earth's faculties, namely gravity, time, and, well, temperature.

I'm sorry you had to go to toy jail. You were framed.

And yes, I slouch on your birthdays. There are just so many of them. And your theme and gift requests are super elaborate.

While we're into true confessions, let me be straight with you: I think what I'm really feeling—the real beast behind my neglectful mothering of you—is contempt. You see, I'm totally jealous. Surely you understand. You get to be the one to sleep in the doll bed, head turned just right so you can open your eyes if you want to check on your sleeping mama. You get to listen to her breathe and hear her talk in her sleep and be the first one she sees when she wakes up. You probably get a Good Morning hug, too, don't you?

My mom tells me I used to have imaginary friends named Saucy and Bossy, but my interaction with them was different because, well, they were imaginary. You're real and tangible. You're so real that I tripped over you last night. I wonder about your conversations with Ellie. I wonder at the stories you've been told, the secrets you've heard, the giggles you've shared. I'm sorry that one day you'll be cast aside because she's so "over it" with you, and that there'll be absolutely nothing you can do about it. But then, the day will probably come when she attempts to cast me aside and say she is so "over it" with me. But we will all know that it's not true—that it can never be true. Because, yes, you might have her attention, her affection, and her obsessive compulsions now, but she and I are flesh and bone united. Her umbilical cord may have been cut from me at birth, but it's still attached in spirit. And while she can (and will) rebel and sass and roll her eyes, we will all know that deep down, she does it from a place of safety; she knows I can (and will) take it. She has known since she looked into my eyes and dropped the peanut-butter-covered spoon off the side of the high chair. She will never be over me, nor I over her. We are mysteriously, cosmically connected, and you are just the first of many who will threaten my standing with her— without success.

So, Olivia, you don't scare me. Okay, there was that one time, but the room was mostly dark and I swear your eyes were following me. I do have a choice to make, though: we can coexist like we've been doing, or I can change from tolerating you to celebrating you. I can stop feigning jealousy or annoyance and prepare for the days when other, more animate people will seem to hold her heart tighter than me. You're a good test run—a kindness from God to ease me into the idea of her divided affections. 'Cause these short years before best friends and boyfriends and husbands and mothers-in-law and children? They're the easy part—the bumper lanes of divided affections. These are the days when I get to watch her try to build new relationships, like mothering you with all her heart, as well as moments when I get to practice remembering that she still has a place for me in her life. I don't want to put my

126

hope in her ability to love me back perfectly, because that kind of hope won't hold. There must be something greater—a Divine Somebody big enough to love me with a better, stronger love than I could ever give.

So I say it's about time I celebrate you, kicky little sidekick. Because nobody wears navy opaque tights and a festooned gold jacket with as much panache as you. Go ahead and enjoy your moment in the limelight. I promise to do my best to honor you during these glory days of yours. Just stop asking if you can use the permanent markers.

Olivia in my lap during Christmas Eve service, 2017. It's a good thing she wore her pajamas because she slept through the whole thing.

22
I'll Give You a Lyft

Abigail Avery

 *Abigail loves a good podcast, Wilson Phillips, and Netflix binges. She is not a fan of most romantic comedies or the stomach bug, both of which have a tendency to leave her somewhat nauseated.*

March 14, 2018

Dear Sir or Madam,

I am writing because I am interested in partnering with Lyft. In order to garner your attention, I've adopted this format of communication in hopes of showcasing my stellar qualifications, as well as pleading my case as to why, despite some minor driving blemishes, you should hire me. In an age when letter writing is practically a lost art form, please allow me to regale you with a heartfelt and thorough correspondence concerning the benefits I would bring to your company. Besides, I found a stamp when cleaning receipts and wrappers from my purse, and thought this letter would give it purpose.

By way of background, I am a higher ed graduate, I've invested time in the workforce, and have four children to my name, solidifying my primary place at home from now until, well, many years from now.

As my family has grown, so has my time in the car: to doctor's appointments, grocery stores, bulk stores, specialty grocery stores (okay, all the stores), in carpool lines, car washes, and gas stations. Because I am an excellent multi-tasker and eager opportunist, it occurred to me that I could continue living my everyday life *and* make money cramming complete strangers in-between the car seats. Thus began my research of qualifications for becoming a Lyft driver and the benefits therein. A cursory Internet search revealed the following company stipulations. I must:

- be twenty-one years or older;

- drive a four-door car, truck, or mini-van, 2007 model or newer;

- have in-state auto insurance;

- have an in-state driver's license;

- be licensed for more than one year in my state;

- have a social security number;

- and have in-state license plates with current registration.

Check, check, chickety-check.

I celebrated my twenty-first birthday near the turn of the century (precluding me from any knowledge of Snapchat filters or use for such words as lit, bae, and/or twerk). Additionally, my 2008 Honda Odyssey is the perfect vehicle for customers who desire that "homey" ride experience, harkening back to simpler times. My no-bells-no-whistles Odyssey excludes the pitfalls of technology and screen time and is everything the constantly entertained and doggedly overstimulated passengers are demanding. They will not be distracted by movies, a navigation system, a pesky Bluetooth, state-of-the-art shocks, nor a fancy tire pressure sensor. Instead, my lovely and practically luxury-grade van (with rubber floor mats and functioning air vents) offers the opportunity to remember what riveting human-to-human connection is like. Beyond a social skills refresher, passengers may also experience using an actual tire gauge! I will be delighted to show anyone with interest how to check the PSI on tires should an opportunity present itself. (Take that, YouTube.) Customers are also encouraged to release their artistic talents by contributing to the preexisting graffiti covering the third-row interior panels. And, as if it couldn't get any better, should I ever have need for an insurance claim, my agency is the bomb. It provides excellent service (I have several of my own testimonies), and I know my agent personally. How many of your drivers can say *that*?

Swelling with anticipation over my new potential employment opportunity with you, my eyes landed on the final requirement: I must pass a background and driving record check which includes no recent traffic accidents or history of reckless driving.

Okay, so there was that Hollywood stop I got cited for a couple of years ago. *However you need to make your ticket quota, officer.* To add insult and a few more depleted license points to an already damaged reputation, I managed to merge into the passenger side of a truck just a few months later. I *allegedly* flattened his tire and busted three body panels. I may not be an auto body mechanic, but I can't help thinking the insurance company was being a bit dramatic—it didn't look that bad to me. The driver was pretty quick to tell me the truck was brand-new. Oh well, "forgive and forget" is what I always say.

Concerned that these two issues might create a slight pause in your consideration, I want to make it clear that I am *much* more than my two-dimensional paper driving record. I am a complex and competent Mom-driver now—a social and vehicular force of reckoning.

First, Mom-driving has prepared me to drive in the most extreme conditions. I have traversed wind, hail, snow, and ice to collect or deliver a child to sundry birthday parties and sporting events. I have never stopped under an overpass with the other sissies because it was "raining too hard," nor did Alabama's worst ice storm in modern history deter me from an on-ramp to retrieve my eldest from having to stay the night at school. I am the defini-tion of complete and full driving commitment to get the job done.

I can also expertly navigate hazardous conditions *inside* the vehicle. I am accustomed to weathering all kinds of nonsense and tomfoolery unfolding around me, including but not limited to: smelly foods, smellier socks, inappropriate voice volume, flying projectiles, repeated horrid music requests, verbal and physical assaults rivaling any reality TV show, Disney-edition carpool karaoke, mindless complaining, endless crying, a penchant for identifying roadkill, and hours of "Would You Rather." Recently, I have been working on my counseling skills as well: listening to story upon story of friendship, playground goings-on, and any number of relational conflicts and bathroom humor. I offer advice only when solicited and do so with much tenderness and care.

I also have zero need for a GPS in my hometown, as I spend no less than three hours in the car each day before noon. I knew shortcuts and repaved roads long before Waze. Accordingly, I can cross the city at warp-speed even during rush hour, and at any given moment know five alternate routes should they become necessary. I perfected these skills while potty training the young-lings, so I have mentally bookmarked every restroom in order of sanitation should an urgent need arise. I am also no stranger to downtime between shifts. Carpool lines have expertly prepared me to power nap, floss, and meditate before receiving my next group of occupants.

I'll Give You A Lyft

As I review the myriad of training conditions I have navigated over the last decade, I submit it as a miracle that my driving record does not contain more incidents. It is clear that my special-ops driving savvy and the benefits therefrom greatly outweigh any minor risk my husband falsely believes I may pose on the roads.

Well this has been a pleasure, and I thank you for your kind consideration as I eagerly await your response. My gas pedal remains respectfully yours.

Warmest regards,

Abigail Avery

23
Live from the Thunderdome

Tweets from My Daughters' Bedroom

Holly Mackle

Holly will forever be remembered as the first person to tell me that one day my ever wakeful, breastfeeding newborn would bound across the room and ask for a cup of milk. In the midst of the Sahara, this information was my oasis.

- Emily

I don't really have a Twitter account. But I do have a hyperactive imagination. The following is based on real events.

 @hollymackle ✔

I'm typing this tweet, listening to a podcast, and cleaning my daughters' bedroom and playroom all at once because: multitasking!

♡ ↻ ♡ ✉   8:56 AM

@hollymackle ✓

Stay behind the velvet rope, people.
Step away from the genius. The brilliance
here is sure to boggle the mind.

♡ ⇄ ♡ ✉   8:58 AM

 @hollymackle ✓

In the playroom. Using my animal tracking skills
full gear. By my reckoning, this spot is where the
crocodile downed the gazelle.

♡ ⇄ ♡ ✉   9:04 AM

 @hollymackle ✓

My oldest runs a toy sting operation. It's a kidnap
and ransom sort of gig. Very undercover. Moderately
dangerous. No one escapes.

♡ ⇄ ♡ ✉   9:07 AM

Same Here, Sisterfriend

HM **@hollymackle** ✓

Oh good. I've been looking for this half-rotten pumpkin.

♡ ↻ ♡ ✉   9:10 AM

HM **@hollymackle** ✓

I suppose I should pause here to be thankful for my daughter's creative spirit, and that a toy is never a toy… (1/3)

♡ ↻ ♡ ✉   9:14 AM

HM **@hollymackle** ✓

…but rather a component of an invention, a serving piece in a delicious feast, or part of the structure of a house. (2/3)

♡ ↻ ♡ ✉   9:14 AM

HM **@hollymackle** ✓

But don't have it in me right this second. rn I have it in me to show you this picture of their questionable grasp on automobile safety. (3/3)

♡ ↻ ♡ ✉   9:15 AM

HM @hollymackle ✓

My daughters love two things: tape and hair-twisties.
Neither for their intended use, but because they
are wonderfully all-purpose. (1/2)

🗨 ⇄ ♡ ✉   9:26 AM

HM @hollymackle ✓

Like vinegar. Or Clinique Chubby Stick in
Bountiful Blush. #twisties (2/2)

🗨 ⇄ ♡ ✉   9:26 AM

HM @hollymackle ✓

Hair twisty count: 6.

🗨 ⇄ ♡ ✉   9:31 AM

HM @hollymackle ✓

Princess Anna's all like, "I've been calling
for help for 127 hours!"

🗨 ⇄ ♡ ✉   9:44 AM

Same Here, Sisterfriend

HM @hollymackle ✓

Yep, this is a great spot for a crumpled
leaf. #falldecor #faildecor

♡ ⟲ ♡ ✉   9:50 AM

HM @hollymackle ✓

Anna's still giving me that Mona Lisa stare.
She's seen things she can't unsee.

♡ ⟲ ♡ ✉   9:55 AM

HM @hollymackle ✓

Hair twisty count: 11.

♡ ⟲ ♡ ✉   10:01 AM

HM @hollymackle ✓

I need there to be a loud honking alarm
noise the next time I attempt to buy a
toy with any small pieces.

♡ ⟲ ♡ ✉   10:09 AM

HM @hollymackle ✓

Maybe a low-voltage jolt as I reach for
more Legos.

♡ ⟲ ♡ ✉   10:10 AM

138

Live from the Thunderdome

HM @hollymackle ✓

Tiny pieces of my soul are shriveling up.
They're beginning to smell like stale pizza.
Wait a minute . . . Found the pizza.

♡ ⟲ ♡ ✉   10:22 AM

HM @hollymackle ✓

Puzzle pieces wrapped in Kleenex and
tied with a hair twisty. Were they playing
meat counter? Jigsaw the Hobo?

♡ ⟲ ♡ ✉   10:24 AM

HM @hollymackle ✓

HOW DOES THIS HAPPEN? YOU PLAY
DOWNSTAIRS WITH MEASURING CUPS
MOST OF THE TIME.

♡ ⟲ ♡ ✉   10:29 AM

HM @hollymackle ✓

And the soul shriveled to one-quarter
of its worth.

♡ ⟲ ♡ ✉   10:31 AM

HM @hollymackle ✓

I will now communicate my feelings
in primitive emoji. :(

♡ ⟲ ♡ ✉   10:33 AM

Same Here, Sisterfriend

 @hollymackle ✓

SOS from 33.5207° N, 86.8025° W

○ ⇆ ♡ ✉   10:35 AM

HM @hollymackle ✓

Is it really my job to prevent you from becoming a hoarder?

○ ⇆ ♡ ✉   10:36 AM

HM @hollymackle ✓

If you become a hoarder, will the documentary portray me as the cause of your poor coping skills?

○ ⇆ ♡ ✉   10:36 AM

HM @hollymackle ✓

IS ONE BORN A HOARDER?

○ ⇆ ♡ ✉   10:36 AM

HM @hollymackle ✓

Why am I doing this anyway? Is this how I want to spend my life?

○ ⇆ ♡ ✉   10:40 AM

Live from the Thunderdome

HM @hollymackle ✓

I JUST REALIZED I DIDN'T MAKE THIS MESS.

♡ ⇄ ♡ ✉   10:41 AM

HM @hollymackle ✓

I think I need a break.

♡ ⇄ ♡ ✉   10:42 AM

HM @hollymackle ✓

Maybe I once fully committed to taking the wrong kid to the doctor, but it doesn't mean I have to commit to this mess. #OSHA

♡ ⇄ ♡ ✉   10:42 AM

HM @hollymackle ✓

Final hair twisty count: 19.

♡ ⇄ ♡ ✉   10:44 AM

141

24
Timehop

Nicole Conrad

Nicole once passed out in the middle of a "Wild West" photo shoot at Dollywood. The family picture remained in her dad's office for years.

It's a ritual: each day I click on the yellow Timehop app with the red notification bubble.

1 year ago today, a photo: two sisters in plaid flannel dresses hug in a doorway. The smallest, Charlotte, has her eyes closed and her brown curly hair is buried into the chest of the taller sister. The oldest, Claire, smiles at the camera as if surprised by her sister's affection.

2 years ago today, a photo: craft supplies clutter the kitchen table in the background. Aunt Katelyn smiles for the camera while holding the Styrofoam ball that Claire is painting as part of her spider art project.

Timehop

3 years ago today: a picture collage of Charlotte, then a baby in a jumper seat. Her reaction goes from confused, to pondering, to happy, and finally a blur of joy as she jumps in response to her first taste of Daddy's famous chocolate chip pancakes.

6 years ago today: Mommy and daughter, baby Claire, dressed in matching cat costumes. Black striped shirts, black whiskers drawn on with eyeliner, and black cat ears. Claire's wide smile revealing her nearly toothless grin.

10 years ago today, a Facebook status: Nicole is looking forward to another episode of *The Office*.

Inevitably, I forward the screenshot to my husband or a family member.

"Look how tiny Claire was!"

"Can you believe how well rested and hydrated we looked before we had kids???"

"They used to get along. What happened?"

There is no mood ring that could pinpoint or decipher the complicated emotions I feel each time I open the app and look at these pictures and posts from the past. I find myself smiling at the snapshots of life and love and mess—hard evidence for future days proving my children did, in fact, have a lovely childhood. But right about the moment my smile can't stretch any wider, I sense a heart-weight sadness that those days are over. Call it nostalgia, call it awareness, call it what you like—time is a funny, fleeting thing, and it's hard not to compare my present to my past, my current

143

self to my former self. My mind fills with a flood of thoughts. *Was life really simpler then? I captured every moment with my first child, did I stop and notice my second enough? Last fall was better than this fall, right? I was busy then like I am now, but I stopped and helped with that spiderweb craft for the kitchen window. Yet, I haven't pulled any of the fall decorations out this year.*

We talk a lot in mommy communities about the dangers of comparison, about not comparing our interior, messy lives to others' curated Facebook personas. But here I am, comparing myself to my *own* curated social-media self from the past . . . and coming up short. Maybe it's because I know the backstory of each image—the constant bickering leading up to the surprise hug, the frustration I felt at purple paint on the kitchen table, the stress of work that prompted the escape to the backyard with my baby on the first day of fall. Those moments weren't perfect either, but they were good.

Smartphones and social media didn't create this wistful nostalgia. You see it in the eyes of the woman at the grocery store as she smiles at your fussing baby and says, "Don't wish these days away. They go so fast." You hear it in the voice of relatives who reflect on how fun it was to buy toys for a one-year-old for Christmas, or who reminisce how tiny she was in that teddy bear winter coat that made her look like a marshmallow. And empirically, a sassy, snaggle-toothed seven-year-old is not as squishable as a sweet, chubby baby, nor does she like to be squished.

I do miss the highlights of the baby years. The awe of "firsts." The unfettered cuddles. I don't miss the diapers. *Oh wait, we still have one holding on.* So, I *won't* miss diapers if we ever get to the end of them. But I don't want to miss the awe and beauty of the growing child here in front of me for the cute toothless grin of the one in the photo. I don't want to mourn mushy hugs to the detriment of finding new ways to show affection to these growing girls. When she was one year old, she was an extension of my body. Her opinions were limited to food preferences and sleep locations. Loving her felt like an automatic response, like loving myself. Now, she is growing to be independent, thinking her own thoughts, and managing (or not managing) her own emotions. She is no longer just an extension of me; she is herself. And loving her is not merely an involuntary motion of my body, to hug or soothe or hold, but so much more. I'm now training her heart toward womanhood, teaching her about healthy relationships, encouraging her to take the right kinds of risks, and holding her hand when she fails. I'm helping her discern the voice of Jesus over the harmful distractions of this far-from-perfect world.

As much as I'd like to relive the memories at times, it's good that I can't. The true awe and beauty of them is the mystery of how that chunky baby, pensively looking at the playground slide, became today's pensive blonde reading about dolphins on her mom's iPad. And how the mom and baby who dressed in matching cat costumes are now the mom and girl who get dressed all by themselves, no longer needing each other for that moment of the day. We are not who we were yesterday, and we are not who we will be tomorrow.

Today, I get to uncover the complexities of elementary school with Claire and the stubborn struggles of preschool with Charlotte. I have enough worries and joys for today without living in the past or comparing today with yesterday. So, I close the app and take a picture of Claire's expression, her mind still absorbed in the daily habits of dolphins, her messy curls sweaty from a day full of recess and learning, her front tooth missing and collected by the Tooth Fairy, who she knows isn't real. Today is today and I choose to stay here in it—complicated and imperfect and wonderful as it may be.

25
Holding

Lindsey Murphy

Meet Lindsey. While she and her husband once dreamed of being internationally-renowned snipers, her maternal affinity for woodland creatures would suggest other career pursuits might be best, as Lindsey cries if she runs over a squirrel. Once, she also made aforementioned husband pull over the car so she could chase an armadillo across a stranger's yard. They were on their way to church and she was in heels.

He did it. He met a big goal—one that stretched him past comfort, and rewarded him with watching *Star Wars*. I mean the real, grown-up version with Jedi, stormtroopers, and lightsabers in all their glory. As he walked up to the car after school, I announced his victory by rolling down the windows and blasting the theme song loud enough to wake the dead. He cracked a smile, but it didn't reach his eyes.

"I hurt my elbow at school today." He held up his arm, brandishing a Band-Aid.

"I'm sorry, bud. What happened?"

He recounted the events of nothing more than rough-and-tumble boy play. Then he paused.

"They laughed at me. All the other boys, and my best friend. They laughed when I fell."

Big, silent tears rolled down his face, and my mama heart crumbled.

I knew this day was coming. We'd made it six years, which was a gracious plenty in light of the world we live in. The day wasn't just about a scraped arm. It marked the end of an era—an era in which he walked through the world genuinely believing that everyone is kind, that all those around him are with him and for him.

I could have turned around and marched up to the school, demanding to know what the teacher did about it. I could have texted the other mama and forced an apology. Goodness knows I've seen those scenes play out over the years in other situations.

But I didn't.

Remembering the many times I myself have needed mercy, I pulled him into my arms and wiped the bitter tears away. We talked about compassion and forgiveness. About using words to build others up. I told him that what he felt was called betrayal. His head perked up. "Like Jesus? Jesus was betrayed too."

Holding

After we got home, he was careful in his actions. He was quick to apologize to his sisters in moments of unkindness. He was kind in response to hard requests. I knew it wouldn't be permanent, as this is a life-long lesson, but there was tangible evidence of a slight shift in his heart toward empathy.

As hard as it was to watch him hurt and hear him wrestle with his feelings, I was comforted in the moments when he took that pain and used it to fuel mercy. I was proud of his maturity—that he knew his Savior understood the pain of loneliness and unkindness too.

As he grows, I know there will be times when he'll need me to stand up and step in. There will be times when he'll need my protection and advocacy. But there will also be times to hold back and let him experience the brokenness of this world within the protective boundaries of our home and family, surrounded by the people who love him the most. This felt like a time to point him to the arms of Jesus, who promises to make all broken things new again.

Holding back sometimes means holding onto the hope of something far greater than me.

26
Horse Bath Aftermath

Holly Mackle

After years of friendship, I'm still not exactly sure what Holly does. Printmaking? Stand-up comedy? Networking? Undercover reporting for People.com? I've decided it's all of the above, and that she goes to Mexico annually to figure out which cool thing to conquer next.
- Cara

I've developed a puzzling skill since having children: the ability to disassociate my mind from my actual surroundings. This happens often when the bitties are experimenting with knock-knock jokes, creating their own remix of the most recent Disney soundtrack, or performing similar repetitive behavior, such as poking me in the face with a foam "Roll Tide" finger. Oh, not to mention attempting to turn me into a human piggy bank by shoving an entire bucket of plastic coins down the gap between the back of my jeans and my derriere. I am present in body, but my mind is absent. And I'm not just talking about when I'm on the phone or scrolling Pinterest either; sometimes I'm even looking at them, but not hearing a sound.

Trouble is, my husband David says this well-honed skill of mine is not just relegated to the children. There are times he thinks we're having a conversation, but apparently I wasn't aware of it.

"Holly," he'll say, all gentleness and self-control, "are you with me?"

Actually, scratch that, he'll say, "Hey, guess what? You just agreed to let me buy a new *car!*"

That. It's mostly that one he says. And before he can fully comprehend how rude I've been, I quickly do some damage control. I smile sweetly and remind him how much he loves me and I point at the little people that are definitely his children. Then I begin to wave my hand around so the pretty ring he put on my finger catches the light and reminds him we're married forever and ever (and ever), and suddenly he's not at all irritated, but filled with delight and gladness at having such a zippy wife. Then he'll ask if he can start dinner, and should he try the new sauce he saw on *Top Chef*? Ok, maybe not that last part, but look, I think I've accidentally disassociated again and *maybe* what's actually happening is just plain ole daydreaming.

But I think it's easier to pretend I have an illegitimate disorder excusing me from dealing with the irritating behavior of others. Namely certain adorable, but relentless, short people under the age of six. Lots of people have illegitimate disorders they tout all the time. You should listen to my three-year-old drone on and on about her peanut allergy. Sheesh. Perhaps I'm developing a Candyland allergy. I bet she hasn't considered *that*.

I can't even explain the scope of what I'm thinking about when I'm not mentally present, but I can assure you (and by you, I mean David) that it's solely about matters of extreme importance, like contemplating how my oldest has come to know a very popular Sir Mix-A-Lot lyric or whether Taylor Swift and Calvin Harris are ever, ever getting back together. Sometimes I wonder where my bitties get this stuff. I mean, it's not like I turn on Bravo and leave the room. Comedy Central sometimes, but never Bravo. *Real Housewives of Wichita,* maybe, but never the *Cops* marathon on FX. This guy from my high school was on *Cops* once. He played the role of perp, not cop. After that, nothing. Sometimes I wonder what happened to him. Like, do you continue to be on *Cops* or is it just a one-shot kind of deal? Did they use the same producers as *The Hills*? What if the very same producers from *The Hills* started their production careers working on *Cops,* driving around in their production van, eating hot Cheetos, popping Red Bulls, and looking for that guy from my high school so the moment they spotted him they could yell, *"Someone provoke him!"*

Look there, see? It just happened again.

I'm pretty sure I know where this skill originated. I can trace it back to the first moment my daughter asked me to play a game called "Horse Bath." This is an imaginary play game, and before you say "Aaaaw," or "Look how fun and creative your daughter is," let me ask you a little something: What is your moral and ethical stance on waterboarding? I give you two minutes, three *tops*, with "Horse Bath." It's basically the new Calvinball (her Calvin and Hobbes training had already begun), except that you get yelled at a lot for forgetting what you're supposed to be doing with your hands. "Horse Bath" made me want to sit very, very still and hope the short people would forget I was in the room.

Well, since you asked, now I'll have to explain it to you. "Horse Bath" mostly happens at bath time, when my oldest child suddenly decides she would like to be a horse. So there she stands, naked as the day she was born, while I'm filling the tub with the substance responsible for what David considers "unusually high water bills," and she says to me, "Mom, I'm a horse." This is apparently my cue to know exactly what to do, but I confess, after all these months, I am still utterly perplexed. Then she goes limp and I'm supposed to dead lift her into the tub because, "Horses don't have arms, Mom." Once inside said tub (which looks to my husband as if it is filled with raw money), she then says, "Mom, you have to bathe the horse." But she's in this weird, hunched over, criss-cross applesauce situation allowing me to bathe approximately 5 percent of her actual surface area. "Here, bitty, raise up your arm."

"*No*, Mom, I *can't* raise my arm!"

Oh, riiiight, because I've already forgotten the quintessential lesson of "Horse Bath." Say it with me: Horses. Don't. Have. Arms.

Who is teaching my child the characteristics of class Mammalia? Remind me to write them a thank-you note.

Also, how do you explain to someone for whom you would walk through fire that you would rather file taxes while sitting on a thumbtack-covered chair than play her game? And all those who have arbitrarily changed the rules of Chutes and Ladders said *amen*.

If "Horse Bath" was limited to bath time, I think I could find a way to deal. Trouble is, the bitties have completely unhindered imaginations—the world is their oyster, our home is their O.K. Corral, and their criteria for what constitutes a "horse tub" are pretty injudicious.

Outdoor garden planter? Perfect!

Large plastic bin emptied of 384 million Legos? Even better!

Sister's crib? Like it was made for this!

Laundry basket full of freshly folded clothing? *How can I be first in line?!*

The day I showed up at the doctor with the wrong kid, I just looked into the face of that politely bemused receptionist and wanted to say, "Horse bath. *Horse bath*, sisterfriend. That's what's happened to me." Because if she knew the rules, regulations, requirements, stipulations, improbable mathematical angles, and the subsequent mental anguish of those invited to play, she would totally understand why I scheduled a babysitter for the kid who was supposed to be at the doctor, why I snacked, pottied, and dressed the kid that should have been home with the sitter, and fully committed to bringing the wrong kid to their lovely, cheerily-painted office. *All in.*

But look (David), at least I'm aware of the disassociation problem. Isn't awareness the first step toward fixing the problem? Or is it admitting you have a problem? Or is it shock? Because I'm definitely shocked by Sir Mix-A-Bitty. And yes, I'm shocked that my husband sometimes speaks to me and I have no idea I'm involved in a conversation. Shocked, I tell you. Just as shocked as the day I realized Nick and Jessica were not going to make it. I'm clutching at my pearls in shock right now and, hey, whatever happened to wearing pearls anyway? Is it not a thing anymore? Don't they say things basically come back every thirty years? And I think the last time pearls were in, I was in middle school, so they should totally be back within seven years or so, and I can certainly wait that long to clutch them because although David may be the epitome of gentleness and self-control, I am the epi-center of unnecessary patience. And seven years really doesn't seem that long when I consider my oldest kid is almost seven and that's practically driving. And I'm not sure I'm ready for that, and somebodycallWilliamFaulknerbecauseIhavenoideahowIgothere-butIthinkitmightexplainathingortwo.

In conclusion, I would like to state for the record that one day I opened the trash can to find this, so clearly I am not the only person to occasionally be overwhelmed by the jar of play money. Even Mr. Fruits-of-the-Spirit has his limits.

27
Memo

Abigail Avery

Abigail always scoops ice cream out of the container in the same direction, evenly across the top, and sets her alarm to an unexpected minute, like 5:43.

MEMO

To:	**My Children**
From:	**Mom**
cc:	**Dad**
Date:	**Feb. 26, 2018**
Re:	**Your Rooms**

As you are aware, per my previous memos, (and since I ~~notified~~ made direct eye contact with you yesterday and repeated this information until each of you repeated it back to me verbatim), our lovely housekeeper Mrs. Deysi came today. Allow me to remind you (since it seems to have slipped your Dark Side-addled minds), she is a kind, gracious, and beautiful woman who has helped our family since before most of you were born. And if years of service get credited in her favor, she was definitely here first. We love her, trust her implicitly, and for some reason, she loves us despite our messes and mediocre Christmas bonuses.

Knowing how special Mrs. Deysi is to our family and how much we value her (i.e. need her to remain in our employ so that mommy doesn't commit arson), I was shocked and dismayed to find the state of disarray in your bedrooms and the playroom. I fear you have begun to rely too heavily on Mrs. Deysi to do her part (cleaning) and have begun to relegate your part (taming your bedlam and wrangling your fidget spinners and Beanie Boos into their designated places) to her. As such, I asked Mrs. Deysi to skip cleaning your rooms and the playroom. This has been a long time coming. I feel it is important that you learn to respect her, and our family, by giving more effort and attention to preparing your spaces for her visits.

I would be remiss as a parent if I did not remind you, yet again, that having a housekeeper is an immense privilege. The vast majority of the world does not have professional assistance in the removal of boogers from windows and proper toilet-paper dispensing—it is over, not under, after all. With this benefit comes tremendous responsibility as we seek to treat Mrs. Deysi with the utmost esteem and reverence. We can show her this by

(1) paying her promptly and tipping her generously with what I have skimmed from your allowance (I warned you about the sass-mouth); (2) thanking her sincerely for her hard work and kindness to our family; (3) preparing well for her presence in our home by having all toys, clothing, knickknacks, light sabers, used tissues, and other belongings put properly in their places; and (4) maintaining her hard work by cleaning up after yourself and others each day. You live here, sweet cherubs of my womb. She doesn't. Act like it.

Accordingly, in each of your rooms and the playroom you will now find the following:

1. An empty box for items you will donate
2. A trash bag
3. Clorox wipes
4. A flamethrower for when things get completely out of hand. (I'm joking. But don't tempt me.)

I expect the following:

1. Every item in your room should be put away *in its proper place*. Pro tip: "proper place" is not a euphemism for being shoved under your bed, under my bed, and certainly not for being flushed down the toilet.
2. All clean clothes should be *neatly* put away in corresponding drawers.

3. All dirty clothes should be *in* the hamper, not beside the hamper. Not on top of the hamper lid. And not in a smelly pile behind the bathroom door.

4. Items that do not have a proper place and can be enjoyed by someone else should be donated.

5. Items that do not have a proper place and are no longer in readily identifiable condition because they have been: repeatedly run over by a car; defaced by markers, permanent or otherwise; served as meal replacement for the dog; or are missing inordinate amounts of spare parts or limbs; should be thrown away *in the aforementioned garbage bag.*

6. Your bed is to be made. Neatly. Hospital corners.

7. The area under your bed should be free of *all* items that do not belong, particularly those things prone to rot and decay such as sandwich crusts, empty wrappers from Halloween contraband, small vermin, etc.

8. All books are to be neatly shelved. Bonus points will be awarded if organized by author and title and/or color.

9. All surfaces—meaning dressers, bookshelves, desks—should be neat and clear of questionable stick or slime.

10. All surfaces, including bookshelves, should be Clorox-ed, Lysol-ed, and anointed with whatever essential oil is on hand.

11. Each room is to be vacuumed *after* being cleared of clutter.

Memo

There will be an inspection upon completion and there will be *no* playtime or extracurricular activities until this list is completed.

Please report any complaints directly to your father.

Don't make me tattoo this list on your arm—Mommy knows a guy from spring break '99. Thank you for your prompt attention.

28
I Dare You

Cara Johnson

 *Cara is an introvert masquerading as an extrovert. She owns a kitten she never asked for, and never leaves the house without a Chapstick—a quirk that has the full support of her favorite actor, Tom Hanks.*

The painted brick gym walls looked like a ceiling-to-floor-length gown. They were baby blue with yellow horizontal stripes and a tan border running one-third of the way up. We kindergarteners used to back up ten feet, run as hard as we could, hold our breath, and jump—with arms outstretched, fingertips splayed like starfish—hoping we'd touch the top of the tan line and achieve greatness.

Perpendicular from the wall was a white line, a crucial part of our favorite game called "Steal the Bacon." In the game, two opposing teams tried to cross the dividing line and steal a bandana (the bacon) from the other team's territory across the gym. But when I played, I mostly focused on two people I really liked: Zoë and Ben. Zoë had the face of a China doll—petite with flawless skin the color of honey. Her crow-black hair had a bit of curl—the kind I'd wanted my whole straight-haired life. She chewed Bubblicious gum, which my mother forbade because it would cause cavities that I would have to pay to fix. If I was lucky, Zoë would tear off a corner of her little pink block to share with me before popping the rest into her mouth, chewing with fervor, and blowing big bubbles that splatted all the way up to her nose.

I thought she was exotic, including her name with its three letters and an umlaut over the e. I thought it gave the impression she was from a place as exotic as her name. Somewhere you only read about in books. Somewhere like Mauritania or Grenada. I added extra curlicues to the vowels in my name just to keep up. She wore three friendship bracelets on each arm, given to her by other Zoë fans, and just as many braided necklaces. With three brothers younger than me, I didn't have any idea where to get string or how to braid it. I was only five! But Zoë knew how—she had powers the rest of us didn't. And for some reason, she was my friend and ally. Most days.

Then there was Ben. He was in my carpool, and some mornings, if I was lucky, we'd share the back of his mom's station wagon—with no seatbelts and my shoulder brushing his on a tight turn. The ride to school was only three minutes long, but I cherished every moment with him and his perfectly brown curly hair, still tousled and messy from the deep sleep of childhood.

A picture of Ben's two-adult, two-children, and two-dog family could have been on a doctor's office poster under the words *"Choose health. Choose vibrancy. Choose your future."* When his dad wasn't in the law-firm-mandated suit and tie, he was going for a run, clad in those thigh-high jogging shorts from the '80s. Ben's mom had smooth walnut hair well-kept in a pixie, and she wore tennis gear every day—the skirt, the white shoes, the visor, the tight-fitting tank—a uniform I now associate with wealth and a few other things I shouldn't. But her wide, welcoming smile and gentle disposition spoke nothing but kindness to me. Ben had one older brother, Will, three years our senior, who wanted very little to do with us green shoots, though he was never mean to us. Both Ben and Will practiced tennis religiously and spent weekends at tournaments—and winning most of them. You know, maybe that's why tennis appealed to me a couple of years later. It was love by association.

But I can't talk about Ben without mentioning Khaki— my friend who was everything I wasn't—because it was she who pushed me to act on my affections toward Ben. Khaki was a shorts-and-oversized-t-shirt kind of girl, one who maybe brushed her shoulder-length hair once in the morning, or maybe not, but didn't really care either way. She wasn't afraid of anything or anyone but wasn't a bully either. Most importantly, I was her friend. *Me.* The one who cried every single day during the first two long weeks of kindergarten, the one about whom my mom and other adults whispered and said, as though I didn't hear, was "shy," the one who would spend most kindergarten mornings before school in her brother's classroom because his teacher was younger and nicer, and mostly because being with her brother made her feel safe.

Not long after I finally stopped crying over leaving my mama every morning, it became *the thing* to dare one another to do something mischievous that the teacher wouldn't detect. The idea started during free play time and involved glue. One of the kids passed word around the class: Whenever we use glue today, spread some all over your hand, let it dry, then peel it off. And try not to let Mrs. Dameron see! As time went on, the Great Glue Dare got weirder: Today, let's all *eat* glue! I touched a drop to my tongue and decided that it was more than enough for me.

But back to Khaki and Ben. On a rare playdate at my house, I divulged my Ben-crush in hushed tones to Khaki, who flew into action trying to get us together. She was also the confidant of Zoë, who, unbeknownst to me until that moment, also liked Ben. "He probably likes her too," I told Khaki. But she was fiercely loyal—to me as well as to keeping the situation private. So she did the most logical thing a kindergarten leader could: she declared a dare.

"The first one to kiss Ben gets to be his girlfriend." *Whatever girlfriend means,* I thought. She said it directly to me, but she had

such conviction and confidence, I assumed she'd said it to everyone in our class. I schemed and thought. *How was I going to kiss
Ben without him knowing? Without anyone else seeing? But with
Khaki there as my witness?* Zoë might have had bracelets halfway
up her arm and nothing but cuteness oozing from her every pore,
but maybe I could have that "girl next door" effect?

Then an idea came to me. P.E. was going to save me.

Earlier that year, I'd learned to call a P.E. teacher "coach"—a
term I hadn't really used before and one that confused me because
*doesn't a coach lead a team and aren't we just playing and not com-
peting, and how serious is this class anyway?* Pretty serious, turns
out. Coach Rick carried the title of P.E. teacher at my school, and
his coaching shorts, polo shirt, and whistle around his neck certainly fit the part. Average but athletic in build, with dirty-blonde
hair cut sensibly short, Coach Rick was mysterious—a man who
didn't talk much and who unpredictably lost his temper. He was
never aggressive or abusive, but his punishments didn't always fit
the crime. We were, after all, twenty kindergarteners who'd been
sitting indoors for too long and needed some freedom to explore
and talk and run.

A few days after Khaki announced my challenge, I saw my
opportunity. Our class was in the gym sitting inside the half-court
circle, and Coach Rick gave us instructions on the day's schedule,
which predictably included stretching, followed by a game. Khaki,
sitting to my right, risked having to run some laps by leaning over

and whispering, "You have to do it now if you're going to do it!" My heart quickened, and I found that my hands were slippery against the smooth gym floor. But I knew she was right. This was the time. As we all spread out and listened to Coach Rick count to ten over and over again with each new stretch, I made sure I was in close proximity to Ben by inching my way—over several minutes—within reaching distance. Ben was sitting just in front of me and to the right so that he could only see me if he turned his head. And then, in what must have appeared to be a very sincere stretch, I managed to graze the back of Ben's shirt with my lips as I reached to touch my toes, coming up with what must have been a very believable cough to detract from anyone who may have seen what just happened. I looked back at Khaki with raised eyebrows and a hesitant smile, and her grin back was all the assurance I needed: I'd won the dare.

Not that I ever spoke of it again. Nothing changed—I still longed to be on Zoë's team in P.E., and I still lived for the weeks when it was Ben's mom's turn to carpool.

Years later, my mom told me that Ben had a crush on me too. How had I not known? Maybe I should have figured it out when he volunteered to sit in the back of his station wagon rather than his usual seat in the middle row. All that whispering and scooting and courage-mustering, and all along the grown-ups had detected everything. They talked about it with each other on their phones, cords stretched from the kitchen to the dining room. They knew all about the glue because the Powers That Be sent a letter home saying, *Please talk with your children about how they should not eat glue.* They tilted their heads to the side and awed at our innocent affections. Of all the grown-ups who knew everything, though, it was Coach Rick who emerged the winner—not because he let us get away with anything, but because he knew when to look away, to let a girl steal a kiss from a boy, and let her win a dare that meant nothing and everything all at once.

29
Four Tantrums Before 9 A.M. — Five If You Count Mine

Holly Mackle

Holly is a compliment deflector. It's one of her many superpowers. I've trained long and hard to get past her superior defenses, but have yet to succeed. You just wait, Holly. I'll have my day.
- Beka

So, my family went to Disney World.

To make it more interesting, I write a garden blog, and before I left I had all manner of friends tell me, "You're going to *love* the landscaping!" Opportunity knocked; I thought I would take a few pictures and write a nice little Disney World Gardens post. That is not what happened.

Oh, I saw the landscaping, but I mostly glanced at it over the shoulder of whichever bitty child had been pulled aside for a talking-to.

My husband David and I are very vocal fans of a specific place in Mexico where children are as welcome as hurricanes. Our concept of vacation does not include twenty thousand daily steps on the pedometer. But as the bitties are into *all the princesses*, we thought it was time to go somewhere a little more magical for a slightly younger crowd.

You see, Disney was very magical. And also very *not*. David and I spent a heck of a lot of time parenting our way through it.

My intentions in vacationing there were good. I wanted to connect with my family. My dream was reminiscent of the commercials: a grinning mom pulls her daughter close while walking toward fireworks and carrying a Mickey-ear balloon. The problem was that nobody told Ellie that she was supposed to play the role of accepting and grateful daughter, and nobody mentioned to Georgia that she was supposed to play it cool flying "no nap."

But, once again, it wasn't about them. They're little. *Bitty*, if we want to get technical. It was about me and my responses— which weren't exactly *mouske-awesome*. Here's the deal: I was made for heaven. I don't mean some puffy white cloud, angels strumming harps kind of place, but a real, physical place where everything is right. *Perfect*, if we want to get technical. And when "the most magical place on earth" doesn't live up to my expectations and doesn't fill my empties, it's just a reminder that I wasn't made for here. This is not my home. And I can plan and pack and prepare the matching shirts, only to have it all fail me in the end because even Disney magic can't fix an imperfect world.

The Mouse doesn't hold up to eternity.

While we could hardly find a moment in Disney World that wasn't perfectly produced or performed to maximize our fun potential, all that magic still couldn't keep Ellie from putting her mouth on every handrail between Dumbo and the Country Bear Jamboree.

Our friends were at Disney with their three-year-old daughter the same time we were there. Catherine, the mom, is kind and levelheaded, gentle and self-controlled. The text message she sent me on the first day cannot be published in this family-friendly book.

I promise I'm getting to my point. If you go to Disney and you look around, everyone's parenting. There are fitful kids and end-of-their-rope parents and much wailing and gnashing of teeth. And yet somehow none of this makes it into Disney commercials. When I started to take notice of the parenting frenzy, I literally saw a grown woman crying as she waited in line for Dippin' Dots. No joke.

Once I repented of trying to get Disney to fill my empties, the mood actually started to get magical. Yes, it could have been that the bitties got used to the routine of the transit/crowds/overwhelm/shared hotel room, but it's likely that it was just my attitude getting adjusted that breathed some happy into our family. Ellie told me the Gatorade there tasted "just like candy." (That's because we weren't watering it down, but who's going to own up to that.) Snow White tickled Georgia and told her she laughed just like Dopey.

Darn you, The Mouse . . . just . . . *darn you.*

If Disney and I had a relationship status it would be "it's complicated." Far more complicated than a few photographed moments. So the next time I get a Christmas card, scroll through some Facebook pictures, or get lost in a beautiful Instagram account, I want to remember what The Mouse taught me: that it is feasible to push a double stroller packed with crying children while also crying yourself. And also that the happiest place on earth doesn't hold a candle to what waits for us in eternity.

So what's your Disney World? Is it indeed a vacation? A job? A dream of something to come? No shame in hoping, but if we need those here-and-now things to bring us the happy, it's never going to be enough. To mix a metaphor, Dorothy was right: there really is no place like home. And for believers in Jesus, this earth will never measure up.

But if you ever need to reach me in this life, look for me on a Mexico beach recovering from my vacation.

30
The Cat Plan

Carrie Brock

If you'd like to meet Carrie, may I suggest a Costco run? I see her there almost every time I go. This friend is a girl boss when it comes to running a household. At my request we once spent an entire playdate comparing notes on how we manage and schedule ins and outs of family life.

I think of my middle child as my sweet Monkey. She laughs loudly, loves deeply, talks incessantly, and moves constantly. And she has a plan. A Cat Plan.

This all started innocently when her preschool teacher asked a question commonly asked of four-year-olds: *What do you want to be when you grow up?* As the typical answers swirled around the classroom—doctor, fireman, teacher, mommy—my little one had a different answer:

"When I grow up, I want to have lots of cats."

I first heard of the plan when she got in the car that afternoon when I picked her up from school. She told me how all the other children had answered the teacher's question, and then she told me about her big dream of having lots of cats.

"Cats, is it?" I asked, intrigued. I then embarked on a few questions to find out more about just how big this plan was. I may have also been looking for a sum total of just how many felines she had in mind.

And, did I ever find out.

All the way home she told me the names for every single cat. They ranged from general names such as Jessica and Maude to more animated names like Fluffers and BonBon. I lost count at seventeen. Also, the names kept changing. Apparently, she was under intense internal pressure to get her multitude of imaginary cats named appropriately and diversely. She passionately referenced all these wonderful cats as if they already existed. She also described, in great detail, the ridiculously huge monstrosity of a climbing tower she wanted for her cats and said precisely which aisle it was located on at Costco. Such a tower would, of course, be required for keeping the cats from turning on each other in boredom.

An important note at this juncture: our family doesn't have a cat. Actually, I am allergic to cats. And we do not have social interaction with any cats either. I don't dislike cats; they are just not my thing. Where did all of my little Monkey's passion come from?

So, back to these cats. And the huge climbing tower. My interest was piqued.

"Mommy, I am going to have a *big* house. The climbing cat tower is going to go in the living room. And each cat is going to have their own bedroom."

"Ok . . . How are you going to buy the house? Are you going to have a job?"

"Nope! No job!"

"What are you going to do?"

"Stay at home with all my cats!"

"So are you getting married?"

"Nope, no husband. And no kids either. I need space for my cats."

Huh.

I gave her a break on the line of questioning. She was only four at the time and still learning that money is effective for buying things.

So I suggested we board a new crazy train of thought.

"Isn't it going to stink in the house with all of those cats?"

"Why, mommy? What do you mean?"

"Well, won't you need lots of litter boxes for them?"

"What's a litter box?"

"Well, it's where the cats go to the potty."

"What do they do in there?"

"Well, you know when we walk our dog outside . . ."

"Wait, what? They do *that* in the *house*? In a *box*?!"

"And you have to clean it out every day. You have to get a little pooper scooper and . . ."

"*Stop,* mommy! That is so gross! I can't do that!"

"So what are you going to do about your cats and their . . . needs?"

"I'm going to train them to go on the potty. And flush too. Because if they don't flush, that would be gross. That's why I need a big house. Because each cat will need its own bedroom *and* bathroom."

Her cats were going to make those cat-food-commercial cats look like they had taken a vow of poverty.

***** *****

Well, the Cat Plan continued on with passion for months. I was impressed by how consistent she stayed—my girl was committed. We were in cat mode all the time.

Then one day after her fifth birthday, I overheard her talking with her brother and sister, saying something about a wing of a house.

"What house are you guys talking about?"

Cat planner: "Mommy! Me and my brother and sister are going to have a stuck-together house when we grow up!"

Cat planner's sister: "Since I'm the older sister I'm going to live in the wing with the tower. All of my art can go there. I'm going to draw all the pictures of her cats. And I'm going to paint all the time."

Cat planner's brother: "I'm going to have the biggest part of the house. My wings are going to be a zoo. I'm going to have a pet tiger. It's better for a boy to have a tiger. And then I'm going to have a lion and a monkey and a giraffe and a zebra. And maybe an alligator. If there's room."

Cat planner's sister: "Since I'll only have my art, I will come and help you take care of your pets!"

It was a rare moment of sibling teamwork and they had made such a fantastically extravagant plan for their house . . . I really hated to ask. But I did anyway:

"So, are any of you going to have a job and earn money?"

Cat planner's sister: "Well, yes, mommy. Remember, I told you. I'm going to be an artist. Oh and maybe I could also be a pet doctor to help all the animals."

Cat planner's brother: "And I'm going to be a zookeeper!"

"So you three are going to live together with all those animals?"

The cat planner had remained uncharacteristically quiet for a full three minutes. Something was up. And then thoughtfully, she said, "Since I'm going to live in a stuck-together house with my brother and sister, I can't have lots of cats. I'm just going to have one. We are still going to each have a wing of my ginormous house. And since it's my house, I will have the middle part. I will put the big cat tower in the middle so that they can visit with all of their pets."

"That's great that you all want to live together! May I come visit?"

"Mommy, I'm going to have a special place in my house for you, with a really nice bed and a big bathroom. And I'm going to get you a really nice kitchen so that you can make cinnamon rolls for me every day because you are going to live with me."

My sweet dreamer included me in her dream.

The talk of the many cats, the one cat, the zoo, and the stuck-together house lasted for a long time, even into the beginning of kindergarten. But then as more fascinating concepts were introduced at school, the cats and the stuck-together house faded from conversation. I thought that was the end of the plan. The end of this particularly, wonderfully, silly idea.

As mid-year into kindergarten and a sixth birthday approached, my cat planner seemed to shift career paths.

"I'm going to train horses."

"Ok!"

And that was pretty much my entire answer, because the extent of my knowledge of horses is that they are big and pretty. Also, I have a respect for the animal, also known as being respectfully terrified of them, especially up close. So I encouraged this newfound love of horses with sticker activity books. This was probably not the most accurate of depictions, but it worked well for a six-year-old with budding horse passion.

"So I'm going to have a horse. He will be a beautiful brown color with white spots and a yellowish-brown mane and tail. And I will brush him every day. His saddle will be rainbow color, because rainbow colors are the best. We will ride around the farm and go everywhere together. He is going to be the fastest horse. He has to run super-fast, because I run super-fast."

I thought we had moved on to horses, but as it turns out some plans are extra sticky. A few weeks after the love of horses began, the youngest was in the car talking about animal week at preschool. And the cat planner, who had continued to be all about horses, was reminded of her previous plan and said, "I love cats. I'm going to have lots of cats."

And just like that, the horses were gone, and the cats were back.

"What happened to the horses?"

"I just love cats. Horses are just too big and smelly. And how are they going to sleep in my bed at night? So, yeah, I'm just going to have cats. Just one or two. Maybe three. Yep. Cats. I love cats. They are the best!"

Holly's Week

SUNDAY

18 Start the week off right with church, exercise, quality time with the fam, and a delicious home-cooked dinner

MONDAY   PRESIDENTS' DAY

19
- Youngest will say her tummy hurts and I will spend first 1.5 hours of preschool wondering if something was wrong with last night's dinner and I shouldn't have sent her to school.
- Call Carrie to wish her a happy birthday, only to realize mid-song her birthday is Friday.

TUESDAY

20
- Will give thanks youngest never got sick but be reminded we are still in cootie season.
- Will remember it's time to plant potatoes . . . only to also remember I never set any potatoes aside in December to sprout eyes.

WEDNESDAY

21
- Call Pamela to tell her this really funny thing only to forget what the funny thing is by the time she answers.
- Date night to Colony House show with hubby. Aren't we young and zippy.

Holly's Week

A rejoinder to "Martha's Month"
from the most excellent *Martha Stewart Living* magazine franchise,
in which Martha lets us in on her calm, orderly, and seasonal plans,
which I'm sure all happen just as she intends.
Even the one where she washes and grooms her cats.

THURSDAY

22

- Remember why we don't go to concerts anymore.
- Pull into school behind my friend with 7 kids again, remind myself she's not judging me, but spend next 20 minutes wondering how she does it.

FRIDAY   CARRIE'S BIRTHDAY

23

- Host fun book launch for friend from Atlanta. Will almost hyperventilate at realization that I'm going to have to launch this book.

SATURDAY   REAL SISTER'S BIRTHDAY

24

- Tear up pantry in quest for leftover Valentine candy. Don't find any and decide I should probably organize pantry anyway.
- Call sister to wish her happy birthday, and also to see if she has any candy. (She won't. Instead, she will have self-control.) Decide to count organizing as exercise.

February 2018							March 2018						
S	m	t	w	tr	f	s	S	m	t	w	tr	f	s
				1	2	3					1	2	3
4	5	6	7	8	9	10	4	5	6	7	8	9	10
11	12	13	14	15	16	17	11	12	13	14	15	16	17
18	19	20	21	22	23	24	18	19	20	21	22	23	24
25	26	27	28				25	26	27	28	29	30	31

Don't forget

32
Rage and Mrs. Meyers

Caroline Saunders

Hey millennials, Caroline is willing to lend you her maiden name for your wedding hashtags—it's that awesome. Batten down your vintage gowns and hoist your man buns: her maiden name is Powers.
#LukeTakesCarolinesPowers #CarolineLosesHerPowers

I need to put this out there: some days, housework provokes a seething rage-monster to crawl out of my soul, spit fire, and lash out irrationally.

Stomping into the bedrooms, I furiously spot the wayward items of clothing strewn across the floor, and I shoot deadly eye-lasers at the socks until they surrender and slink into the laundry basket. Actually I just pick them up, but the eye-lasers part is true. My husband can confirm this because sometimes he must dodge these very lasers after inexplicably leaving every single kitchen cabinet door open. Why would a person do that?!

We cannot even discuss the beard hair on the bathroom sink. We cannot discuss it.

I nearly drown in massive piles of laundry, but I fight valiantly against the overwhelming waves of t-shirts and single socks, and prevail. Rage is helpful in this way. I take a load out of the dryer to fold and put the freshly washed load into the dryer, finally remembering the thing I forgot days ago: Clean out the lint trap! *"Argh!"* Rage Monster Me yells. *"Why is my brain so stupid!"* This will surely end in catastrophe someday, and I will be shamed on the Internet by nameless, faceless trolls.

Unfortunately, the lint trap is so hauntingly full that the lint particles have joined together to miraculously form an actual Muppet. "I've been trapped in here for days!" the Muppet squeakily laments, and this makes me furious. *Why must I always be the one to free Muppets in this house?* Then I remember that I do all the laundry. *Why does no one else do the laundry?* Of course, I am conveniently disregarding facts that are not conducive to my rage: 1) my husband and I have consciously divvied up the household chores, and yours truly got the laundry; and 2) my kids are two and three years old and are only capable of dirtying clothes. However, I am certain you understand me when I say *my rage has no use for logic.* I take my aggression out on the Muppet, and I crumple him up and toss him into the trash without a moment of remorse. *Get out of my sight! You disgust me!* At the loss of the Muppet, the children wail and gnash their tiny teeth, and I hand them each a fistful of crackers. It is hard to wail when you have a fistful of crackers.

My laundry hysteria confuses me for a while, so I stand in the kitchen forgetting how I ended up there and wondering what I should do next. This is not uncommon. It's my tendency to ping-pong back and forth between tasks until all things are 23 percent completed, and I collapse in exhaustion, unable to finish a single task but equally unable to be okay with it. *Not this time!* I proclaim nobly to myself. *I will not ping pong!* So I strategize: should I clean the bathrooms? *Ew, no.* Dust? *Haha. Dusting is for fancy people.* Vacuum? *Yes, perhaps the noise will drown out my angst.*

For a moment the whir of the vacuum feels like a balm to my soul, and it's satisfying to see the machine devour the one thousand pounds of cracker crumbs that live on our floor. Emily Henderson says to decorate with texture, but I imagine the grit of Goldfish underfoot is not what she had in mind. At some point in the vacuuming, my daughter and son (now crackerless and back to wailing) each attach themselves to my legs, and I power through like a bodybuilder on leg day.

Productivity-induced adrenaline pumping, I decide to clean the countertops. My three-year-old daughter wants to help, but this is made difficult by the fact that she's three, and the fact that she is deeply committed to wearing socks on her hands. Nevertheless, even my inner rage-monster has her maternal moments, and with the careful use of a stool and Mrs. Meyer's Lavender Multi-Surface Cleaner,

Adelaide helps. The cleaning continues, poorly, and as my motherly patience begins to wear thin, the counters endure my scrubby frustration and I sniff the lavender scent in hopes that I'll chill.

Now of course it's time for dinner, something I remember with a deep growl. "Why did I clean the counters when dinner prep will inevitably get this place messy again!" I bellow like the monster Grendel in *Beowulf*, while Sock Hands scampers off to unfold laundry.

Imagine how victimized I felt upon reading the pork tenderloin label: *Cook for approximately 30 minutes and then allow pork to rest for 5 minutes.* The audacity! I shake my fist at the sky and shout to no one, "The pork shall not rest until I do!"

Oh, pork privilege! I cannot bear it. Because it's not right, okay? The pork tenderloin doesn't get to sit all day in juicy apple-ginger marinade and then demand five minutes to rest. It's reminiscent of College Me on spring break, exhausted from sitting on the beach all day and needing a nap, blissfully unaware that one day, imaginary lint-Muppets would send flames out my eyeballs and that I'd envy a pork tenderloin. I want to soak in apple-ginger marinade! I want to rest for five minutes! The last time I did that, my three-year-old non-napper violently patted my face the whole time, saying, "Shhh Mommy! Goodnight, Mommy! I love you, Mommy!" until I gave up, kissed her delicious face, and set out to scrub the bathtub aggressively.

Rage ain't pretty, but in some stages of life, she's the only hope for housework.

Part V

Gotta Be Your Own Friend

*Pro Tip: Pack your favorite afternoon snack
so when the contents of the lunchbox come home
uneaten, you won't be upset. You'll just say,
"Oh look, someone made me a snack."*

33
Over Thirty Dance Team

Holly Mackle

When I get bored, I like to text Holly pictures of my children submerged in the plastic ball pit at a local indoor playground. Nothing says "you are my tribe" like evoking a good old-fashioned germophobic flare-up in a sisterfriend.

- Laura

Every Friday at precisely 9:45 a.m., you can find me in one place and one place only: Dance Jam. This is the dance/hip-hop/bet-you-didn't-know-I-like-a-little-gangster-rap exercise class at my local gym. As I've invited friends to join me for this remarkable event, I am often met with odd looks, disdain, raised eyebrows, and the most common kickback, "I could never do that."

"It's not a tryout or a performance," I reply with that *c'mon, man* kind of attitude. "Wait," I change my mind, "Scratch that . . . it *is* a tryout . . . it's a tryout for *happiness.*"

I've never understood people who run on a treadmill or plod along on the elliptical. Do these people not know about Dance Jam? I feel as if I should make a public service announcement: "Attention, thirty-somethings! Are you aware that you can work out without being bored stiff? Need to reconnect with your younger, firmer self? Want a place to join in an activity alongside people who like to bust loose and have fun? Remember those days when you were a little girl in dance class and everyone was *boom-hit-pow*-ing in unison under the watchful eye of the slightly authoritarian dance teacher? Want to do that again?"

Okay, so before you start heckling, let's just discuss, in a calm rational manner, the following point-by-point analysis of how my workout is infinitely superior to yours.

1. Dance jam is supremely beneficial to one's mental health.

How else would I have gained awareness of Mariah Careyoke?

And although the real reason for the mental boost probably has something to do with, well, you know, science and brain chemistry and endorphins or whatever, let's not forget the primal feminine power of assembling a large mass of women in a mirror-walled room and allowing them to feel, for one hour, like they've still "got it."

2. Dance Jam is cathartic.

There's a certain segment of the female populace that gets fired up at the words "All Hip-Hop Friday." They love to be in that room, stomp-stomp-clapping in sync like a team, everyone releasing their inner sweat-drenched Sasha Fierce. It's fun. It's electrifying. It's cathartic. If you are not *yet* one of these women, let me tell you the little secret we know that differentiates you from us: *ain't nobody looking at you, girl.* Did you hear that? Ain't nobody watching you. Just you. In the mirror. And since ain't nobody watching, you are free to get down to that funky sound.

3. Dance Jam is a little high-energy pep talk that goes a long way.

If you come to class unmotivated by your childhood Rockettes obsession, fear not, the instructors are supremely competent in the art of the well-timed motivator. And they'll call you out if they can tell your heart's not in it, but they also understand the mama stuff. They know we just wiped something mysteriously sticky off the edge of a counter not five minutes before we left for class and that we don't need to think about that right now. I sure could use a Dance Jam instructor in my ear all day as I'm going about my daily tasks. In fact, dibs on that idea . . . I'll make an app that plays in the background of your life. *This is so my* Shark Tank *idea.*

Baking muffins? Dance Jam app hears the clink of the mixing bowls and a female voice shouts out, "I really want to believe—make me believe!"

Putting on makeup? "Respect the body you came here with! We're not auditioning for the Laker Girls."

Giving a kid the side eye? "You owe yourself some drama."

Picking up toys? "Squat lower. It's almost shorts weather and we've got some make-up work to do."

Waiting on the crossing guard? "I can visualize it . . . an explosion of glitter."

Walking briskly because you're late for school pickup? "Squeeze your buns so somebody else will want to!"

In line at the dentist? "Gimme your best boy band pose!"

Washing your face before bed? "End the day with some sass. Let's lower the heart rate but not the attitude."

4.   Dance Jam breeds cultural intelligence.

Dance Jam is responsible for a good degree of my pop culture currency. In my household, the only other adult conversation contributor is my husband, and his pop culture tidbits are generally items of a slightly questionable nature. Not to mention they're mostly picked up from the early '90s frat house—certainly not from a source that would help with beneficial, up-to-date, pop culture references. No favorite gown at the Oscars. No celebrity baby names. And since I dropped my people.com habit, I find Dance Jam extremely advantageous as a breezy way to keep up with my favorite performers: "Love doing squats to this TSwift—is she still with that British guy from *The Night Manager*?"

Moreover, Dance Jam attendees effortlessly combine high-brow musical preference and pop culture currency. I have probably never written a sentence that my husband and half our friends would disagree with more. But Dance Jam attendees will nod their heads if I say Justin Timberlake *rond de jambe*. Or I'd probably get a high five if I said I'm waiting on a P.M. Dawn/Ed Sheeran mashup. When I go, I am among my people. We have all, at one point or another, worn out a *Jock Jams* tape. We are Destiny's Children, and this is a bond I can never share with my husband. There is a real-world scenario in which I have spent entirely too much time thinking about this. Our supper club makes fun of my musical taste with great regularity, but then I tell them to go eat another Werther's, because, clearly, I am the only one who knows how to have a good time.

5. Dance Jam feeds friendship.

With all my enthusiasm, you might be tempted to think that I've been attending Dance Jam for quite some time. That is not the case. I am relatively new to the class, and as a result, I'm still meeting people. I do have one very best friend, Meg, who comes with me—and there's pretty much nobody I'd rather dramatic-reach-for-nothing alongside. But beyond Meg, I'm still in the process of getting to know people. I owe my parents one very big thank-you note for this lesson: *if you want to make friends, you've got to put yourself in situations where it might happen.* "Must be present to win," as my pastor says.

Before Dance Jam, I was a Jazzercise aficionado for several years. When it came time to change gyms I was super sad to leave what had become my Jazzercise family—people I would not have met under normal life circumstances, people who made my life richer. Never underestimate the power of an exercise class or any gathering of women that might appeal to your interests. Just show up.

I do have one request, and this friendship spot seems like the place to air it. You see, while I would like to befriend you, fellow Dance Jammer, I think we should reserve our newfound friendship for before and after class. During class, I'm really going to need us to obey the laws of the dance window. Everyone please remain neatly spaced—mama needs her hula hoop of personal, perfectly distanced dance floor.

6. Dance Jam is for life.

Since I'm a planner, sometimes I look around the room at Over Thirty Dance Team and wonder, *So what happens with this? Do we all just continue to age here? Will we eventually only just march in place and talk about our ailments between songs?* Because if we stick together, that could be pretty awesome . . . we can simply continue to raise the age limit. "Seventy-Plus Dance Team" sounds pretty much like perfection to me. Maybe we can have a kicky name. My vote: Thundercats.

The music will keep up with our aging. Katy and Jason and Justin and Taylor? They can fight it all they want, but they're just going to age right alongside the rest of us. So they might as well hunker down, brace for crow's-feet, lower the volume but not the sassitude, and figure out how we can all grow gracefully into the geriatric age of hip-hop.

Because whether I'm thirty-seven or sixty-seven, I'm going to need this, people. Whether my littles are clinging to my knees or calling me from college, I need to be part of something beyond myself. And the best way to scratch that itch is to find a place to let loose without fear of judgment, to have fun with friends old and new, and to be reminded I still have some fire left in me. Lace up and stretch out, Thundercats. We've got work to do.

And some day in my future, I'll say with confidence, "Buckle up, kids. Grammie's about to teach you how to pop and lock."

This piece is dedicated to my sparkling Dance Jam instructors Jo-Anne, Nicole, Cristina, Denise, Megan, and Leslie, and to my effervescent Jazzercize teacher, Michele. You are never allowed to retire.

34
On Greige

Nicole Conrad

Nicole HATES sidewalk chalk. The fact that her kids even know what sidewalk chalk is means she loves them sacrificially.

I took a nap. That was my fatal mistake. If it weren't for my sleep greed, none of this would have happened. My husband and children were also taking a lovely Sunday nap, but that's beside the point. Inevitably, disaster struck while *my* eyes were closed.

I awoke to the sound of a fire alarm while everyone else continued their undisturbed respite upstairs, completely negating the purpose of a fire alarm. The wood floor in the kitchen was flooded with water, which was still gushing from my open refrigerator door as if it had a vendetta to settle. The pool in front of the fridge increased at a visible rate. The fire alarm blared from the basement, deigning to turn off when the water reached it and shorted the circuit. Yes, water had seeped through the floors of my kitchen and was pouring from the ceiling of the finished basement like one of those soothing rainforest showers they have at spas. I was not soothed.

Warped floors, ruined ceiling tiles and ductwork . . . it was a mess. A mess I certainly wouldn't have been able to pay for apart from homeowners insurance. As an exercise in futility, you should try explaining the concept of insurance to a child under the age of seven. Now, whenever I tell my daughter, "No, we can't afford to buy you a pony,"—and this is a literal statement that has come out of my mouth—she tells me to call the insurance company and have them pay for it. *If only, sweetheart.*

Repairing the damage meant partially replacing the wood floors in the kitchen and then refinishing everything to match—a process that would take nearly a month. The repairs were so extensive that we had to move out, which landed us in a pet-friendly hotel with two kids and a dog for most of that time. Free advice: bathing a dog in a pet-friendly hotel bathtub is not the glorious after-school activity you think it might be.

At 7:45 a.m. on the morning we were supposed to move out of the pet hotel and back into the house, I received a text from the contractor: "We are painting the kitchen and downstairs bathroom today. Do you want the same color?"

I'm sorry, what? Come again? Tell you a paint color? Now?

I must have missed the earlier conversation in which he had told me they would be painting. Painting was not on my radar. Considering the dozens of samples, hours, and bathroom-floor crying sessions it took to choose a floor stain, impulse decisions are clearly not my thing. But I also knew this was my opportunity to have someone else paint for me as well as *pay for it*. (Important background information: my husband and I don't paint well together. For us, it's the fastest ticket to marital counseling.) This would be a kitchen and a bathroom: rooms with nooks and crannies that require the dreaded taping and cutting-in. I had already broached the painting subject before the water damage happened. The whole downstairs and the halls in the stairwell and upstairs are the same goldeny-camel color and covered in smudgy kids' fingerprints and crayon art. My wheels began to spin and squeal like I was in *The Fast and The Furious: Tokyo Drift*. I thought, *If we pay extra to have the contractor paint the living room, then that's almost the whole downstairs. Once hubby sees the nice clean walls, he'll sign off on helping me paint the halls and stairwell this summer . . .* and *voilà!* Home renovation complete!

"I'll text you a paint color for both rooms by nine o'clock," I responded.

Minutes later, I was a woman on a mission as I entered the nearby paint store. I grabbed fifteen paint swatches in a flurry and then asked the man working at the counter for assistance. "I'm trying to pick a neutral for my kitchen and living room. Can you help?" What I should have said was, "Can you give me Benjamin Moore's Revere Pewter?" And all my Pinterest gals said amen.

He directed me to some very nice "accessible beiges."

I smiled politely and took the samples. But in my head I was saying, *This is a kitchen. Not a doctor's office. I don't want your bland accessible beige. I want a neutral with personality. I want my walls to say, "I'm neutral but it's not because I lack panache. I'm classy. I'm sophisticated."* I needed greige.

For the uninitiated, greige is grey-beige. An excellent choice for the modern but traditional home. Goes well with ship-lap or exposed piping, neither of which I have in my home. A perfect greige welcomes you in and makes your furnishings look better than the Pier One they came from. There are an infinite number of blogs and Pinterest pins devoted to the beauty of greige and how to pick the perfect shade. Did I consult them? No. No I did not.

I slapped my swatches on the wall and quickly eliminated. *Too purple. Too blue. Too dark. Too brown. Too meh.* I sounded like my toddler when I try to dress her in the morning.

And finally, the last swatch standing was Mindful Grey. Even the name was soothing. This was no "accessible beige." This was thoughtful, contemplative, self-aware, *mindful* grey. I texted the contractor, raced back to work, and confidently announced the color to my husband.

"Grey? Really?"

"It's more of a greige," I responded with a knowing air of condescension.

I texted my mom, who replied, "That'll look so nice and clean with your white cabinets."

I confidently showed my friends. "It says grey, but it's really not *grey* grey. You know?"

I eagerly returned home after school to see the change. I bounded up the garage stairs and quickly opened the door from the basement. I peered around the corner, hope gleaming from the corners of my eyes, and saw it.

It was . . . grey.

I know I'm slow to adjust to change, so I took a deep breath and held my reactions in check to wait for a second opinion. David and my daughter Claire came home shortly after. My face was a hopeful question; Claire's was confusion and then horror.

"What happened to our walls? Who painted them *grey*?" She dropped her school bags as though sucker-punched.

As exasperating as Claire can be, she is my id: my truest self in six-year-old form, full of heightened emotions and limited impulse control. Her words were exactly what I feared to say aloud. We both cried.

And my husband? His confusion was immense. He had said yes to all my requests and had returned home to receive his due of grateful adoration. And the very thing I said I wanted was the very thing that reduced two of the women in his family to a puddle. In response to his confusion, all I could muster was, "We're not grey people. We're warm-gold people."

Well, David liked the grey. I was right when I had schemed that David would see the newly painted walls and enjoy not seeing fingerprints and crayon marks. I tearfully texted pictures to friends, who also loved the grey. My mom said, "It's great and there are no fingerprints. Be happy. If you had wanted something more brown, you shouldn't have picked a color called grey." *Touché, Mother.*

I went to Pinterest to see what colors I had previously pinned before I decided to wing it at Sherwin-Williams. To my chagrin, every single pin was grey. I liked it on Pinterest. I liked it on HGTV. I was revolted in my own home. I suddenly felt *crazy.* It's as if I had gotten rid of all my favorite jeans and replaced them with paisley palazzo pants, only to discover I don't like paisley or palazzo pants. Was greige my paisley palazzo pants?

It's been three months since the greige debacle. My husband still looks at me as though I'm crazy when I try to explain the difference between the grey I got and the grey I envisioned. Invariably he says, "I don't think the word 'grey' means what you think it means." Recently, after coming home from a week spent with family for Thanksgiving, I returned to my kitchen and for the first time really liked the color. I still haven't hung much on the walls. I'm too afraid of marring a blank canvas.

I do long to live in a home that is soothing and peaceful. I want to create a place for my family that is inviting and stress-free.

Same Here, Sisterfriend

When I watch a house being revealed to a family on *Fixer Upper*, I believe that the beautiful new home with all its soothing colors and shiplap will fix every problem and conflict. Their laundry is magically done and put away in color-coordinated kids' rooms, their shoes and coats hang themselves in the beautiful mudroom, their white Carrara marble kitchen island is a gathering place for people and not junk mail. Their lives are better than mine.

But I know that's a lie. The greige is a blank canvas on the walls of a house—my family is what makes it a home.

35
Retreating

Cara Johnson

For years Cara has been a most trusted friend and editor. That is, until she told me her pen name, should she have to choose one, would be Jackie Strider. I am currently re-evaluating both our friendship and working relationship.

When I tell others about it, I say it's my "Semiannual Personal Retreat," but let's take off the elbow-length white silk gloves: the time I spend in a hotel room by myself for twenty-four or thirty-six or forty-eight hours twice a year is the very nectar of my sanity.

It all began when I tried to go to a women's leadership training conference when my son was three and my daughter was fifteen months old. I was going to do something for myself! Hone skills! Make connections! Pee alone! It was destined to be great.

But.

You know how these things go. In order to leave, you do all the same work you normally do, but you pack it into less time so you can have a few days off. You move hell and high waters to secure childcare—a.k.a. your mom—because of course this is the weekend your husband has to work. You buy and cook food ahead of time so your kids won't give your mom the verbal "This yucky!" beating they give you on any given night. You spend six thousand hours typing up detailed, helpful, ridiculously long, slightly compulsive instructions so that at bedtime the kids won't say, "Mommy lets me sleep with ten billion lovies at the end of my bed," or "Mommy says it's okay to never ever brush my teeth." You pack your bag and you sleep on the couch so your mom (who arrives the night before so you can leave early in the morning, bless her) can have your bed. And you tell yourself, *This will all be worth it, girl. Just stay the course. A two-hour car ride alone and adult conversation and brain stimulation and eating meals without sharing your food and sleeping without the hum of a monitor await you, princess. Do your Cinderella chores now and the Fairy Godmother will work her magic and you will return from the ball refreshed and in love with your prince and little woodland creatures all over again.*

On top of all that, I just *knew* God had another reason for me being at the conference, something bigger than the leadership training itself. Maybe I was going to make a connection with a writer who could spin me on a path to impact. Or I'd meet an older, wiser woman who would want to take me under her wing and mentor me. Maybe I was going to meet my new best friend in the form of my roommate, a woman from church whom I didn't know all that well. Let's just say my expectations were to the moon, and I was sure I could fly there with the little wings my Fairy Godmother was going to affix—sparkling—onto my shoulders.

For the past six weeks we had been invaded by sickness (both kids and me) and night fears (my boy) and sleep deprivation (all of us), so *it was time* for Mommy to get away. Those six weeks took six years off my life. I could almost taste the metallic blood from my metaphorical teeth being kicked in. Maybe I'm being melodramatic, turning a trying month and a half into a graphic physical beating. Or maybe I'm just being honest.

It was then, when my cheekbones still felt bruised, that I saw the hand—unrelenting—ready to punch me again.

At 4:00 a.m. on the morning I was supposed to leave, my boy cried out. *He's just afraid*, I thought. *No problem. I'll just bring the couch cushions into his room and sleep there and he'll go right back to sleep.*

Let's just say my mom-o-meter miscalculated.

The boy moaned for the next hour and a half through his sleep and woke up complaining that his ear hurt—something he'd never said before. My heart winced from the load of bricks dumped in it, but I was undeterred: I'd set up a doctor's appointment first thing, we'd get him some medicine, and I'd be on my way just a little late. No problem.

The doctor confirmed that the boy did have his very first ear infection, poor thing. But I should have known something else was up when he walked into the waiting room and curled up in the chair like a cat. And when he couldn't sit upright in the patient room. And when he kept complaining of his stomach hurting once we got in the car to head to CVS for his meds. You see where this is going, don't you? But I didn't. I mean, a doctor just looked at him and said it was only an ear infection! Onward we pressed to the pharmacy so I could get home, get him settled, and leave him in the entirely capable hands of Mimi.

We weren't five minutes from the doctor and thirty seconds from me telling my husband, "I mean, he's not throwing up or anything so I think I'll still go," before The Sick One said from the backseat, as if on cue, "I'm going to throw up!" And before I could do anything to help, there it was: vomit all over his lap, shirt, and car seat. And it was seventeen degrees outside so I couldn't exactly air out the car on the five-minute drive home. Free advice: There are lots of reasons to choose a pediatrician close to you—this is one of them.

Another brick in the heart. And a new plan: *Get there tomorrow, just a twenty-four-hour bug, surely. I can still enjoy one day of the retreat and make all my preparation for being away pay off.*

But after only sleeping from 1:30 to 4:30 a.m., operating a vehicle from Birmingham to Atlanta the following day seemed like a liability, and the thought of being at a table with people I didn't know well and trying to have some semblance of logical conversation carried zero appeal. I didn't need hugs and sympathy from lovely, believing women. I didn't need to share a room with anyone. I didn't need to drive to Atlanta to get a "break." After nearly an hour of indecision because of my people-pleasing issues, I decided to raise the white flag and not go.

But not going felt like cutting off a limb. I'd worked for months to orchestrate my two-and-a-half-day absence. I'd planned and cooked and typed and rearranged, and not going felt like a giant waste of *so* much time and energy. *What was the point?* I tearfully moaned to my husband Phil the following morning. There was no reward for my hard work. It just wasn't fair and wasn't what I planned and wasn't what I needed.

But God knew that too.

It wasn't long before Phil suggested I get a hotel for the day while he watched the kids—for twenty-four hours. (I know y'all are like, he suggested *what*? And while he really is all kinds of awesome in the husband department, I'm 99 percent sure his suggestion had more to do with the crazed look in my eyes and the aggressive aging happening to my face rather than his own selfless heart.) The thought of a hotel room thrilled me, and then—the thud of guilt: *I can't leave the kids. I can't leave him with sick kids. That's not fair to him . . . and so indulgent of me.* But he wouldn't have it, and as I began to wrap my head around the reality of so many hours to myself to do whatever it was that was life-giving, I almost felt that giddy lump you get in your throat when things are too good to be true. So around noon, I was sent away with a kiss, leaving the kids in the most able hands of their daddy and looking at a day and night to myself.

My gut was to be productive: work out and run errands for the family and work on putting together the family photo book I was about four years behind on. But I quickly realized that those things weren't going to be life-giving. Hotel days are for pulling away, processing, being quiet, being alone, healing—things I really can't invest in at home. But what would the day look like? It had been so long since I'd chosen something for me and only me that I wasn't even completely sure of my favorite color anymore.

My uncertainty lasted about five minutes until my brain got the message that I was really, truly alone with no one else's agenda, at which point I generated a quick list of options. On that freezing day, I found my feet soaking in hot water for a pedicure; I ate sushi for lunch, watched part of a *Jimmy Fallon* episode, took a perfect nap, shaved my long-neglected legs, wrote while sipping hot (hot!) coffee, and left my hotel room as little as possible. My heart buoyed.

I'm sure the conference would have been encouraging and challenging. I would have made new friends and connections and learned deep truths about Jesus. But I also wouldn't have slowed down, experienced the lightness of being alone, or rediscovered that my favorite color is brick red.

Retreating

And that began my twice-a-year time away, alone. Sometimes it's a hotel in town; other times my husband takes the kids to his parents' for the weekend while I get to stay in my own home and my own bed and let me tell you—alone time in your own home when you have young kids is *weird* and *wonderful*. I rarely advertise my retreat because then I'd be tempted to meet people for lunch or walks and overschedule my downtime. I rarely play music or watch TV because silence is just so hard to come by.

And it's almost never easy.

I fight guilt on the front end and feeling overwhelmed by reality on the back end. When I leave or they leave, the ugly cry ensues.

I cry because my dearest loves are away from me.

I cry because I feel guilty and relieved all at once.

I cry for all the things I haven't had time to cry about for the past six months.

I cry because I don't let myself cry most days.

And when the cleansing is done, I shake hands with myself and say, "Nice to meet you. Want to hang out? What would you like to do today?" And it's there in the solitude that I find my sanity and God and the other sock that's been missing for months and my favorite pint of ice cream to eat all by myself.

36
Madame Ladye Queene

Lindsey Murphy

David and I met Lindsey and her husband when they bought our first house. As far as friendships go—the rest, as they say, is history.

I recognized in myself at an early age a tenacity that I long felt was more burden than virtue. Surrounded by Christian women my whole life, I noticed they all seemed to exemplify the quieter virtues of godly living: meekness, gentleness, kindness, quiet service. My fierceness and fire seemed to disqualify me from any chance of actually walking in a manner worthy of my calling. I spent a great deal of my teenage years desperately trying to chameleon into what I thought I was supposed to be.

Until Joyce.

I had anticipated Joyce Herring's AP English class for years. She was revered and beloved among the students, and my senior year heralded the appointed time for me to take my spot in her class. Perhaps the most elegant person I have ever encountered, she quoted Edmund Spenser and G.K. Chesterton in the most honey-sweet Mississippi accent and wrote in the finest calligraphy with her highly favored fountain pen. (Every year, seniors would flock to stationery stores to buy their own pen. Mine is purple.) She would sit at the front of the class each day, softly glowing with love and passion over the text she was teaching. Instead of the typical catty nicknames bestowed upon teachers, we reverently (and secretly) referred to her as *Madame Ladye Queene.*

But for all her elegance, there was an undeniable fierceness about her that stirred something deep within me. Her brilliance was clearly evident, her zeal for life and literature unmistakable, and her strength undeniable. And yet, she had managed to take this fire and channel it into gentleness, humility, kindness, and a quiet spirit. While on a school trip I remember watching Joyce with her husband in an airport as he advised her how to navigate a task she had accomplished many times prior, and rather than using her potency of intellect to tear him down and assert her competence, she swallowed her pride and responded with a grace that built them both up. Her humility and deference made them stronger, and though she would never have guessed how closely I was watching, her example has served my own marriage well.

I was enthralled and drank in every moment with her. I even had the good fortune of traveling to England and Scotland on her annual literature and church history trip, where it was clear that her admirers weren't limited to a classroom in Memphis, Tennessee. What made her sparkle and delight so? The longer I watched, the clearer the answer became: Jesus.

You may be familiar with the sirens of Greek mythology—how they lured sailors to their deaths by drawing them to rocky shores through their irresistible songs. I learned in early adulthood the beautiful contrast between how two very different heroes, Odysseus and Jason, were able to sail safely past them.

As the story goes, when he approached the siren's territory, brave, fearless Odysseus ordered that his crew plug their ears with beeswax, yet had himself bound to the ship's mast with open ears. He wanted to hear the song for himself. He told his men that no matter how much he begged, they were not to release him. The crew did as he said, and when they neared the area where the sirens dwelled, Odysseus strained to escape to their song, and the crew bound him all the tighter. Only as they sailed far from the sirens and their songs, were their ears unstopped and Odysseus unbound.

Jason, however, took a much different approach. Knowing that he, too, would pass by the sirens, Jason brought Orpheus on the journey. Orpheus was famed for his incomparable music—like that of the gods. None could match the beauty of his voice or his lyre. When Jason's ship neared the islands of the sirens, he instructed Orpheus to play his most beautiful songs. Orpheus played, and the sirens sang. But the music of Orpheus was so beautiful that the songs of the sirens held no appeal for Jason and his men. They sailed safely past without injury or even a memory of the siren's singing.

You see, my whole life I had been like Odysseus. I clawed against my own desires, my own flaws, and my own fire because I had felt compelled to. Joyce, however, kept her eyes fast on Jesus.

* * * * *

Years later, when I learned of Joyce's cancer diagnosis, I felt the very wind kicked out of me. When I finally calmed from crying, I looked at my husband and told him, "She's going to do this well." And she did. Six months turned into three gracious years. I don't even pretend to believe that she walked every one of those moments in perfect contentment and faith, but the glimpses she gave showed the same fire and grace I had always known. She listened to the same song of grace and it stayed her and sustained her, even through a dark, dark providence. She left behind a legacy of tenacious faithfulness manifested simply and profoundly through a life lived well in submission to Christ.

When I remember Joyce, I often think of the last scene in *Dead Poets Society* when the boys stand on their desks and tearfully proclaim, "O captain, my captain," as their beloved teacher leaves. I don't have a desk to stand on, but my purple fountain pen sits next to me as I write and mother and love. I pray my life is a testimony of her legacy. I pray I might one day be a pillar of spiritual mothering for another in the same way that Joyce was to me. She showed me how Jesus can use this fire to warm, not burn, and that even in the scariest waters, He is my strength and song.

Well done, Madame Ladye Queene. And thank you.

37
Confessions

By Anonymous (Because this $#*t Is Real)

I'll let Anonymous answer the wedding hashtag question herself: "I've never been on Twitter, so I don't understand hashtags. But I do occasionally enjoy hash browns, and if I'd had a wedding breakfast, I might have liked to have had hash browns served there. On my honeymoon, we mainly ate waffles, because the lady who ran the B&B where we stayed made them every morning."

Dear Fellow Mother,

Forgive me, sisterfriend, for I have sinned . . . against God, against you, against my child, and against most established parenting standards.

And it's been way too long since my last confession.

First, from an early age, my child has watched far more TV than the American Academy of Pediatrics recommends. I just can't seem to get dinner cooked without it. In fact, I have often treated the guidelines as more of a daily quota than a daily maximum. "Have we watched our obligatory hour yet today? Only thirty minutes so far? Then by all means, let's cue the next episode of *Wild Kratts*."

Then, I always forget snacks when we go out. Not a couple of times—*always*. I'm sorry my child voraciously consumes the grapes you bring to the park for your own kids.

Speaking of forgetfulness, I also fail to keep a stash of age-appropriate, on-the-go, kid-friendly activities in my purse. "Child, would you like to build a teepee with mommy's credit cards while we wait in line at Jiffy Lube? Or draw with lipstick on this old receipt?" I've had babysitters show up better prepared than I am to engage my child in thoughtful, creative, and educational activities.

Admittedly, I will forget about our playdate tomorrow unless I set an alarm on my phone. Putting it on my calendar is not enough—I literally need the phone to vibrate and shout at me in order for me to remember.

Supposedly, motherhood makes you a safer driver, but that's not the case with me. Sometimes it's all I can do to focus on whether the light ahead of me is green or red. And I regularly tune out my child completely while driving. "Mom, did you hear what I said?" No child, I did not.

I regularly forget that my child is now old enough to hear and remember the things I say about other people.

Lord, have mercy.

You were deceived the other day when you saw me walking calmly out of the kindergarten yard with a sulky child in tow. When you witnessed my daughter deliberately disobey me, I think I gave you a "chuckle-and-eye-roll," as if to say, "Kids will be kids." But I was not laughing. I was not calm. I was full of rage, which I bottled up in front of you and the other parents for the sake of public propriety. But once in the privacy of our car, I unleashed the full fury of my tongue against said child for what could be considered "normal" five-year-old antics.

Honestly, I need to repent to my child for my harsh tongue almost every day. Some days, I repent so much that I start to get tired of asking for forgiveness.

Christ, have mercy.

At times, I envy you because of your job. I envy the money you earn so that you can pay someone else to clean your bathrooms once a week. I envy your smart work wardrobe and your flat-ironed hair. I envy your opportunity to leave the house and do something at which you excel. I don't excel at stay-at-home parenting—I've suffered more failures in this calling than in any other job I've had. But perhaps you have envied me too, for the day I was at home when my daughter first rolled over, for the time I was able to stop everything and snuggle her all day during her first ear infection, or for the way I'm available for school pick up. Seems like we moms can never win on this one.

Some days I cry because of loneliness.

I wish I'd stopped at mere envy. But no, I've hated you at times. I hated you for getting pregnant so easily when we had been trying for years. I hated you when I saw how you immediately regained your size 2 figure just a month after childbirth. I hated you for having a freezer full of breastmilk while I was scraping by with formula and endless pumping. I hated you for making your child a homemade Thomas the Train costume for Halloween when I could barely remember to order one on time from Amazon. And I hated you the other day when your kids were so polite and obedient at the grocery store. On all these occasions, I hated you for having something or achieving something I didn't. I started to see you as my rival rather than my friend. I forgot we were in the same boat on the same daunting journey.

Lord, have mercy.

Have you ever hated me? Maybe the time I told you my baby slept twelve hours every night? That ended when the two-year molars grew in. Or maybe the time I told you my daughter prefers roasted cauliflower to French fries? That's really more a matter of her taste than my doing. So, I obviously have some things to boast about, but there's usually more going on behind the scenes than I share. I'm sorry for being so quick to show you my successes and so hesitant to reveal my messes.

Perhaps my greatest transgression is that, in committing the sins of envy and hatred, I have refused to see you for who you really are. In indulging hateful envy, I chose to know you only as a stereotype: the mom who has it all together. By doing so, I didn't offer you a place to be vulnerable. And I wasn't vulnerable with you either. I didn't let you see *me*. Instead, I turned my back on the potential for friendship. For this, I am truly sorry.

Why this confession? On one level, it's an olive branch to offer you the real me in friendship. Because we won't be able to extend the support and encouragement we so desperately need if we're not honest about the aches and struggles. And heck, I just really need a friend for this season—someone who can walk this path of motherhood with me as we sing *Kyrie Eleison* over each other. And I don't mean Mr. Mister's 1985 hit—I mean the liturgical prayer: *Lord, have mercy. Christ, have mercy. Lord, have mercy.*

Of course, on a deeper level, my need for absolution exceeds your capacity. Even if you accept my confession and love me with all you've got, you still can't take away the mess in my heart. For that, I run to Jesus. Because He *does* have mercy on me. He doesn't just sweep my mothering failures under the rug. He bore all of them—and all my shame—on His shoulders when He went to the cross. And when He died and rose again, He took the record of wrongs against me and laid it on Himself. He gives me a new heart and a new name and covers me with all His glorious, shameless perfection.

38
For My Mom. So She Knows.

Cara Johnson

Sometimes Cara and I lose track of time discussing our mutual affection for her chocolate chip scone recipe.

As a child, it was magic being around you in the kitchen—maybe because I got to eat scraps of food, but it probably had more to do with being the only girl among three brothers. It was the place to keep company with you without anyone else wanting to join in; the place to learn about food and cooking and life and womanhood and the news. Do you remember that tiny TV in the corner to the right of the bay window? It was only a little bigger than a box of saltine crackers. *Oprah* or the news droned in the background, sometimes zooming to the foreground if something was particularly newsworthy. The O.J. trial, for instance. Or Princess Di's accident.

For My Mom. So She Knows.

I have no idea how you felt about me hanging around the kitchen. Now that I'm a mom, I wonder if maybe you wanted that time to yourself. But you let me in. You'd give me little jobs and then I'd ask you about eighteen questions to make sure I was doing it right. For years, I practiced the famous ketchup-mustard-brown-sugar sauce for your homemade chicken nuggets. I sweetened the tea by counting the white saccharin tablets in my palm, dropping them in, and watching them magically dissolve as I stirred until tiny tornadoes formed. Sometimes I'd get to stir the cheese packet into the hot macaroni and my mouth would water just looking at those electric-orange clumps. I'd be sure to leave it a little lumpy so I could spoon myself the noodles with extra cheese when we got to the table.

I'm sure my "help" was painfully slow and often hazardous. But you invited it.

Then one day you gave me a *real* job. You handed me the box of rice-in-a-bag and let me take over from there. *"Really?"* I asked. "Sure," you said, as if it were as natural as blinking.

As Stephen plunked on the piano in the next room, you'd call out, "F sharp!" and then *laaa-ed* the right note for him as he played through—one key at a time. Your years of vocal performance training had given you the gift of perfect pitch, but the rest of us were still working to catch up with you. Another brother set the table, quickly tossing the cornflower-blue plastic (read: easy to clean) placemats into position, anticipating the mountain of plates and silverware and napkins you'd soon bring over.

I measured the water into the pot and set it to boil, lid on to speed up the process—something I'd picked up from watching you. As I waited for the steam to shoot out the sides of the lid, I read the box over and over so I could memorize it and impress you by not even needing the instructions:

Four cups of boiling water. Unopened bag of rice in water. Boil 10–12 minutes. Remove and drain.

Four steps. No big deal. Except instead of "unopened bag," I read "opened bag." And it didn't make sense for a plastic bag to go in boiling water anyway. I was determined *not* to ask you eighteen questions about how to do this one simple (grown-up) task, so out came the scissors and in went the rice, swirling in the bubbling water, free as a school of minnows. Immediately, I felt a tingle of heat in my cheeks. I grabbed the box with a sinking feeling, swallowing hard before asking, "You don't cook the rice *inside* the bag, do you?"

I'll never forget your reaction—a mixture of reality, grace, calm, and confidence—the combination I love about you to this day.

"Yes, it stays in the bag . . . did you already pour it in?" you asked, walking over to the stove. Seeing my mistake, you let out a quick, "Oh, shoot!"

"I'm sorry. I must have read it wrong," I started, eye on the pot.

For My Mom. So She Knows.

"Well, that's okay. We can probably just cook it like that. You didn't realize. Don't worry about it."

Your words were like taking off a too-tight belt. You took over from there while I started filling your glass and Dad's with ice—but not out of shame, out of usefulness.

My husband says that you're one of the three most practical people he knows, but you were completely impractical when it came to serving dinner. Having four school-aged children, I would've thought you'd go buffet-style every night on paper plates. Serve 'em up and dish 'em out kind of thing. But you didn't. Nearly every night, you served food in serving dishes—mounds of homemade mashed potatoes sprinkled with paprika (to look pretty, you said), bowls of steaming broccoli, and platters of homemade meatloaf that you'd kneaded with throbbing-cold hands. All those dishes created twice the cleanup, but it brought beauty to the ordinary and honored us as children by trusting us to pass breakable dishes. The need to pass food (to the left!) and serve those near us created a living lazy Susan that taught life lessons without words. We had to communicate and help and choose our own amounts, and it was all so loud and chaotic and wonderful. The thirty minutes when we stopped other activities to share a meal together each evening were some of the best minutes of my childhood, and I'm guessing some of the best (and maybe worst) of your motherhood.

I want to remember the "rice moments" now in my own kitchen when, wanting to help, little fingers fling flour across the

223

floor because they're learning the ins and outs of a whisk, or when they want to set the table and it takes fifteen minutes because they want to open each napkin to its full capacity and "decorate" each place setting with rocks from outside. And while I'm not quite ready for serving dishes at the table, maybe once my kids are plunking out their own versions of "Hot Cross Buns" and using placemats as Frisbees before dinner, I'll find myself digging in the back of my cabinets for the beautiful serving dishes I got for my wedding and think, as I so often do, *Mom would love this.*

39
Delete These When I Die, but Not Before Then

Holly Mackle

Holly is so smart, quick-witted, and capable that I am nearly convinced she's Lorelai Gilmore. I'd like to pitch myself as her quirky sidekick Sookie, but I can't cook, and also . . . we don't live that close and have never actually met—but that's beside the point.

- Caroline

You know what I mean . . .

You've got them, I've got them, we've all got them.

Photos on my phone I can't bring myself to delete:

This is from a series of shots Georgia took called Unsuspecting Mama at Unflattering Angles. *There are approximately 129 of them, with slight angular differentiation. The thought of deleting them makes me tired and also concerned that, in a flourish of frustration, I will accidentally delete my entire Photo Stream.*

The shoes I bought because I wished they matched my life. I kept them in my closet for about two weeks and petted and fed them at intervals, but then decided they do not go with my life right now and returned them. I cannot bring myself to delete their photo.

Me parenting.

I don't know what's happening here, but I'm impressed (and concerned).

Where we parked on vacation. I'd hate to forget.

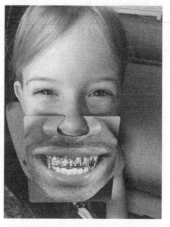

My future WWE champion

Because the holidays are hard on us all, my friend Josie created the most amazing "anonymous" Christmas card I have ever seen.

227

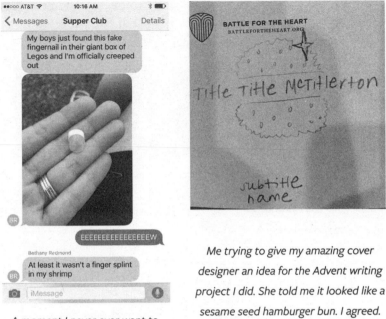

Me trying to give my amazing cover designer an idea for the Advent writing project I did. She told me it looked like a sesame seed hamburger bun. I agreed.

A moment I never ever want to forget, but try to every day.

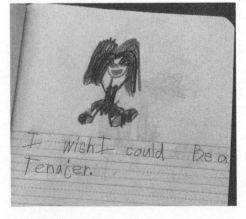

What I look at when I lose sight of what real fear is.

This is my husband, David.
The blackberries were literally
as big as his head.

This is David's epitaph. It was so nice
of Babylon Bee to write it for us this
far in advance.

The items which I once had
to convince Georgia were not
necessary for church. Yes, that's a
cape, a loaded doctor bag, and the
chandelier from the tent.

A present I bought for a friend.
Long live Etsy.

A small portion of the annual Halloween haul parent tariff. And there's a new president so the tax rate is higher this year. It's not personal, it's politics.

This is from another one-hundred-plus series of shots, called How They Painted the Preschool Hallway.

Things I See

■ **What you did there**

One of those memes that makes me wish memes weren't anonymous, because I want to shake this person's hand.

Somewhere in between Proverbs 31 and Tupac there's me.

Same here.

And finally, this is of a game called salon. It looks more painful than my general salon preferences.

Maybe someday I'll submit these to the Getty Museum as an exhibit called *Unedited: A study in the Dynamics of Motherhood.* Because, in this case, I think Oscar Wilde is right: life totally imitates art.

Part VI
Sisterfriends

Pro Tip: Make phone calls from a closet. Kids can smell when you're on the phone. Yes, the call will resemble a hostage situation. "I don't know how long I have. Can you get me out of here?"

40
Is My Mascara Running?

Holly Mackle

A farewell hug in two parts.

Last night you sat on my couch and let me cuddle her. Her baby-soft, tender skin smelled of lavender, hope, and promise. Her eyes searched my den, wide awake but content, looking for contrast or a glimpse of the awe-inspiring ceiling fan. At six weeks, she isn't napping well, and you asked me what I remembered of my daughters when they were still filling diapers and fighting naps, trying to figure out how to help her let go and rest during the day. Me? I'm now the one being asked for help? How did I get here? It seems just yesterday I was the one begging for the magic fix from my mama friends ahead in age or stage.

Same Here, Sisterfriend

Hoping to stir a memory or discover the scrap of advice, you looked at me, perhaps wishing for that book, that forum, that guru. I wish I had it—I would have given it to you so gladly and freely. But to "fix it" would be to sell you the snake oil of the latest and greatest instead of the forever true. Mothering can be confusing because these days, real solutions seem more elusive than vapor while the books—which are tangible with pages to turn and pour over and underline and turn again—are full of empty promises.

My best advice? Embrace the end of yourself. The sooner the better. If you're not quite there yet, know the time will come. And when it does, welcome it. Wrap your arms tight around the complete emptying of yourself to such a degree that you really learn—maybe for the first time—that God's love is sweetest in our weakness. Open yourself to the mercy and the means of children as one of His methods of showing us how big His love really is.

* * * * *

When my book club sisterfriends met to discuss the Mindy Kaling book I told you about, by the time the night was over we were tipped back in our chairs, sore from full bellies and full hearts, our makeup all smeary from the tears—mostly from laughing—that we'd cried as we sat together.

What happens at book club runs far deeper than whether or not we actually discuss the book, which (spoiler alert) is not that often. No, what's happening at book club is about connection, community, friendship, shared experience, and reminding each other that it's okay to laugh our way through the trickiness and perilous day-to-day-ness of this mom-life. That kind of laughter binds hearts together, because it's the laughter of transparency and resilience, and of authentic hearts fully committed to loving our families and friends.

It's the kind of laughter I can't drum up or put on—and it works its magic and makes me feel like *I'm not alone.*

Every time one of the contributors emailed me a story for this book, it was like a life-giving gulp of refreshment. For me, their transparency was a gift from God. It was the grace of soul-comfort that I'm not the only one who feels like she's stumbling along—a bit of freedom from the myth of perfection in motherhood.

For me this journey has been a big ole reminder of just how important my people are. They buoy my heart, they help me keep moving, they are my reminder to inhale when it feels like I'm doing Miss America hair all the livelong day . . . just trying to get one more pin in place during a squirming, waving, is-she-crying pandemonium circus situation. Seriously, my sisterfriends remind me of what matters. They remind me of who I am as a daughter of the Most High King. I sure hope I can be that kind of friend in return. Curating this book has given me an even greater appreciation for the kindness of God in placing these women in my life. I don't want to forget or get over the sweetness I've found. I don't want to overlook that the God who designed us gave us laughter as a means of arriving at connection and support within our communities.

My friends are awesome, but (sorry ladies) we're really not that unique. I'm convinced friends like this are everywhere.

Have you found yours?

If not, let me share from our mom experiences that the journey we're all on is way more fun with friends. Whether or not we admit it, individual sheer determination only gets one so far. We need God and each other. Will you let other mamas sit beside you along the way? Can they be there for you when you feel afraid or emptied or as though you don't qualify for the role? I hope you'll find another mom and give her an excuse to have a good laugh. Put this book in her hands. Start your own book club. Be a book club sisterfriend to another mama in need of a couple hours away from the trenches, a few gut-busting laughs, and a reminder that we are all mothering right alongside one another, so we might as well have each other's backs.

And if the answer is yes—if you have found your people— it's pretty great that God would provide such awesome friends, huh? Let's give thanks together. I don't know about you, but I want to ride out this crazy adventure alongside my sisterfriends. It is a wonderful thing to know and be known.

We need each other, friends. Let's get to the business of loving our people well, and letting them love us in return. In those moments of real connection with sisterfriends, where each lays her heart bare and shows the messy-beautiful of what it looks like to live this mom-life with dependence on God, well, those are holy moments. So drink them in (preferably with a nice cabernet), toss your head back, and have a real heartfelt laugh while your lovely sisterfriends do the same.

Shout-Outs

As I have mentioned a time or twelve, this book was inspired by my book club. And beyond being super fun and kicky, my book club is also handy, especially around Christmastime. That's because every Christmas we have a big party with festive beverages and pigs in blankets and a little game we call "Favorite Things Dirty Santa." It's Oprah-meets-sanctioned-theft among dearest friends, and you get lots of tips and ideas on an array of interests, all for fifteen dollars or less. I've discovered my favorite cleaning products, candles, books, CDs, and journals all during this game. As an ode to Book Club, we thought we'd recreate the experience for you here, dear readerfriend, and give you our lists of most favorite things. Because we like nice things and know you do too. Enjoy!

Holly

Garden Variety Newsletter It's not about gardening. It's what feeds my voracious appetite for the interesting by centralizing all the smartest and most fascinating stuff from the Internet into a manageable digest. Where else can you find all the best stuff from *Bon Appetit*, *New York Times Magazine*, and *GQ's* websites? Emily and Mallory are *on it*. And they'll tell you what not to miss so as to remain an informed, educated person.

Voxer It's the spot. If you're all, "What's Voxer?" I will take a very deep breath before I accidentally shout, "Only something that will change every relationship you have FOR THE BETTER." Oops. *Ahem.* It's an app, there's a free version, and it's a game changer. You can talk to your people and hear their voices without having to ring their phones and make them think someone's fallen from a tree and broken a limb. Way better than texting, and don't even think to ask me, "Isn't this just the same as voice memo?"

Cara's Chocolate Chip Cream Scones Recipe

(Were you hoping it was going to be in here somewhere?)

Ingredients:

2 cups unbleached all-purpose flour

1 tbsp baking powder

3 tbsp sugar

½ tsp salt

5 tbsp chilled, unsalted butter, cut into ¼ inch cubes

¾ cup chocolate chips

1 cup + 2 tbsp heavy whipping cream

Whisk together flour, baking powder, sugar, and salt in large bowl. Using a pastry blender, quickly cut in butter until the mixture resembles coarse meal. Stir in chocolate chips. Stir in heavy cream with fork until dough begins to form (about 30 seconds). Transfer dough to countertop and knead by hand just until it comes together into a rough, slightly sticky ball, 5–10 seconds. Roll into a ball and then flatten into a 1-inch thick disc. Cut scones into desired size and place on ungreased cookie sheet. Bake 425° until light brown, 12–15 minutes.

Beka

Bone Broth Collagen There are two types of people: those who function well enough in the morning to eat a well-balanced breakfast, and those who gulp scalding-hot coffee as they use their purse as a lasso to drag their kids into the car. I am of the latter variety. By the time I finish my second round of school drop-offs, my hands are shaking because I have shot so much caffeine through my empty digestive system that I can literally feel my blood vessels vibrating. And then I started dumping a scoop of bone broth collagen into my coffee on my way out the door. Not only does it help boost my energy by providing me with 10g of protein I do not deserve, but it's also great for my hair, skin, nails, and joints. Basically all the things that started deteriorating the moment my first child was conceived.

Mac Mineralize Concealer That's what I use, but I don't expect you to be so financially irresponsible. There is no shame in the Wal-Mart cosmetics aisle. Buy a color a shade or two lighter than your skin tone. Great, now let's talk application. Look at yourself in the mirror. Tilt your chin down until all your chins have come out of hiding and are embracing each other. Look at the bags under your eyes. (Do you love me right now? I can feel it.) Take your concealer and trace those two matching lines that look like inverted replicas of the Gateway Arch in St. Louis. Now break up the family reunion your chins have been enjoying and lightly blend your concealer with a sponge, a brush, your ring finger, a baby washcloth—whatever is on hand that is soft and doesn't smell too bad. Enjoy the five years I just returned to you.

Trader Joe's Dark Chocolate Almond Laceys Cookies Shhh . . . just trust me.

Cara

The BaconBoss If you like bacon (which you should if you are breathing), this little sucker might just change your life. Personally, I've taught my kids to chant at all three meals, "Bacon makes it better!" Cook one minute in the microwave per strip of bacon, and all the fat drips to the little moat at the bottom so it's easy to pour off when you're done, and voilà! Breakfast side dish! Snack! Sandwich layer! Note: you'll need to Google "Pottery Bacon Cooker" because someone decided the name needed to be tamed. But as for me and my house, we will raise our fists and shout "BaconBoss!"

NASA and ISS (International Space Station) Instagram Embrace your inner nerd and start ogling some of the most jaw-dropping photos and videos you've ever seen. Nothing makes me seem smaller and God seem bigger in a shorter amount of time than viewing a photo that looks like gorgeous modern art and reading that it's actually hundreds of thousands of galaxies. I pull up the account page any time I hear another toy bucket being dumped on the floor and am feeling especially existential.

A Cordless Leaf Blower This lightweight wonder isn't just a battery-powered way to clear your driveway of leaves in the fall. It's straight-up therapy. Having one of those days where you can't seem to get a moment of peace and quiet? Let your kids play in your car and enjoy the white noise as you leaf-blow the driveway. It's five minutes of easily justified "you" time, and if you're lucky, your arm will be slightly sore the next day, which means you can count it as exercise.

Pam

Gluten Yeah, I just said gluten. If you have celiac disease or some legitimate form of gluten intolerance, I'm sorry, I don't want to offend you (and I wait with you in eager longing for the new heavens and new earth where we can break bread together again). But gluten needs a shout out because wheat's wonder protein has gotten a bad rap lately. As a registered dietitian and avid home chef, let me state for the record that gluten is *amazing*—the way it produces that glorious soft chewiness in a good French loaf, or those feather-light layers in a croissant, or that perfect *al dente*-ness in homemade pasta. I'm getting shirts made, who wants one: I ♥ gluten!

Audiobooks Last autumn, I decided I wanted to read *Middlemarch*, but I'm a slow reader, and when was I ever going to find the time to get through all seven-hundred-plus pages? With the audiobook version, I could listen to a little chapter here and there while walking home from school or scrubbing the bathtub or chopping veggies for dinner. I got through that book in two weeks flat. So if you like to distract yourself from the mundane—while still accomplishing the mundane—this is the way to read books.

Rooibos Tea A little bit sweet, not too bitter, delicious with milk and honey or just on its own, this caffeine-free South African red tea is my go-to autumn and winter cozy drink. I recommend sipping some while you knead a loaf of bread and listen to *Persuasion* in your earbuds.

Lindsey

Brookside Chocolates These little gems are a staple for all my parent-teacher conferences, which in my case looks a lot like ugly crying in a locked bathroom while googling local school scores and tuition fees. The bag boasts all sorts of healthy-ish words and natural-looking pictures, plus they're made with real fruit and dark chocolate, so really, you might as well be eating a salad.

BBC's *Poldark* *Downton Abbey* lovers, harken to my call. *Poldark* is everything you need to fill the void left in the absence of Cousin Violet's quips and Mary's snide remarks. Drama! Costumes! Smoldering lead character! (Oh my!) Plus, it's set on the stunning cliffs of Cornwall, leaving me with a deep longing to fly to England after every episode. I have to remind myself after binge-watching YouTube recaps that this place and these people don't actually exist. But still, *I want to go to there.*

Pamplemousse LaCroix I got hooked on this stuff during my last pregnancy, and I think I'm in it *fo' lyfe.* Yes, you might initially feel like you're drinking bubbly gasoline, but it's amazing once you get to know it. Interestingly enough, I recently learned it's the hipster drink of choice. I don't know if this makes me look cool or desperate, but I'm putting a check in the "on fleek" box for good measure. *Viva lá pamplemousse!*

Caroline

Diet Dr. Pepper with Vanilla from Sonic Let's talk about 4:00 p.m. It's the time of day when my kids' heads spin all the way around like owls, and they either fling themselves off raised surfaces or Velcro their bodies to my legs and chant nonsense while I fire off SOS texts to my husband. What does this have to do with Diet Dr. Pepper with vanilla from Sonic? The pursuit of the holy nectar necessitates that the owl-children and their hostage (@me) get out of the house for a bit. Highly recommend.

245

May Designs Journals These journals are so profoundly cute I have to breathe into a paper bag every time I venture onto their website. Adorable, modern prints, a zillion personalization options, and I kid you not, you can even make the lines on the inside pink. Before you make your selection, you *will* pass out from decision fatigue at least seven times, but it's all part of the process, so you must embrace it. Just make several designs, save them, and buy every single one when there's a sale.

SMEG Toaster When we moved into our new house, some of my besties gifted me with a mint-colored retro toaster as a housewarming gift. One of those besties is named Megan Morris, so the SMEG became Smegan Smorris, naturally, and it's the joke I tell with every morning bagel. *Smegan, please toast my smorning bagel.* I am incredibly pleased with myself for coming up with this joke, my family adores the fact that I can't stop telling it, the bagels are delicious, and the toaster brightens the countertops. Everyone wins!

Emily

Distressed Bralette by Lizard Thicket This sultry little number caught my bloodshot eyes one sleep-deprived summer day. I had purged my underwear drawer of all droopy boob bras (a.k.a. nursing bras) and was overcome by a feverish urge to feel pretty—not at an underwire level but more of a shelf bra bounce. If you have man-children who require endless hours of outdoor romping, this bra is for you. You can go from park day to Pilates to "Well hellllo lover!" in one day donning this sporty yet sexy gem. So if you're feeling frumpy, scoot on over to the Thicket and let that mom-bod rock.

Great Value Rocky Road Trail Mix Twenty-three ounces of a decadent dessert and trail mix hybrid, consumed best after wine o'clock in the afternoon. Chocolate, marshmallow, caramel, and a few nuts. Not recommended to share. Best eaten alone while hiding in a dark closet far away from children. And if you fail to follow these instructions, your saving grace is the label "trail mix," which deters most small humans or hangry husbands. Friends, don't be fooled; there is way more heavenly than healthy in this satisfying snack.

Abigail

Ellie Holcomb's *Red Sea Road* Album Lather. Rinse. Repeat. For hard times, for good times, and for every time in-between, this album should be a staple in your playlist. Laced with truth and Ellie's edgy voice, each track helps change my self-talk and reminds me of all that is right, good, and trustworthy. Oh, and my kids love it, too, which is a huge plus in my book since people keep telling me that much of my '90s rap therapy isn't, ahem, kid-appropriate. Sigh.

Cherry Blossom Pet Spray by Animal Pharmaceuticals Confession. We lost our mind recently and got a puppy named ~~Regret~~ Sherlock. He is adorable, pees everywhere, chews anything, and three-fourths of my kids love him. After a few weeks of adorable puppiness, the stench of animal began to settle into our house like my in-laws after the birth of our first child. Coincidentally, I took Sherlock for his first professional grooming where I was convinced they broke open a jar of anointing oil from biblical times. He smelled incredible: clean, fresh, slightly floral, and exactly zero percent canine. And it lingered for *days*. It is the Chanel No. 5 of pet sprays, and all pet owners should have some.

Laura

Norwex Descaler So apparently there is this Norwegian cleaning product company called Norwex, which is steadily bringing its planet-friendly, chemical-detesting existence into our fine country. And they are all about getting my family and me out of the current grimy situation that is our house. For instance, they believe shower doors don't have to look like frosted glass unless they were actually frosted. For years, despite multiple attempts with a variety of products, our shower door remained foggy. But Norwex Descaler confidently walked up, gave it a wedgie, and took its lunch money. Be forewarned, a downside to a clean shower door is that the world sees the condition of your tile and grout. It also severely limits your ability to hide in the shower from your kids.

Ibotta When I tell you this app allows you to earn money on the items you purchase, I am also going to ask you to fight the urge to picture an extreme couponer getting paid twenty-one cents for buying three cases of Purina Dog Chow when she doesn't even have a dog. Ibotta will not turn you into this woman, but it will greatly increase your chances of chest-bumping your cashier when she hands you the receipt, because later you will take a picture of that receipt and make some hollah dollar bills. It's an intuitively organized app where you select rebates for items you already buy (hello frozen pizza, Oreos, and hot dogs). Conversely, it will regrettably not create a sudden respect for the food pyramid. You can cash out at twenty dollars, take your spoils of victory, and go buy a Norwex Descaler.

Carrie

Bullet Journal Yes, I have joined in on the craze that is sweeping the nation. It's called the Bullet Journal, and if you've never heard of it, you are just a quick Google image search away from more ideas than you will ever need for journaling. The Bullet Journal (BuJo for short), created by Ryder Carroll, has a standard format, with ever-evolving infinite variations. The beauty of the BuJo is that it combines my need for organization, lists, and schedules with my paralleled need for creativity. I almost love it more than my iPhone.

Fitnessblender.com This is the best (*free!*) website for those who love an at-home workout. It's run by a couple who gives great instruction, variations for all fitness levels, and workouts of different types and durations. Their encouragement, realistic conversations during the workout, and enjoyment of what they do is evident in every video. Daniel and Kelly are some of my new trainer friends, and I miss them if I don't see them for a while. My favorite part? They end every workout with the words "Workout complete!" which I can then go check off in my bullet journal.

Stitch Fix Imagine a box that arrives with five pieces of clothing, customized to your fit and style, without having to lift a finger (ok, one finger to click SHIP). When I see my box from Stitch Fix sitting on the front porch, I feel like a child on Christmas morning. I plan a special retreat to my room to carefully open it, and am consistently filled with wonder and excitement to see what my stylist has picked out just for me. Having *loved* most everything I receive from her, I am completely convinced that she has a spyware device installed in my closet. I can keep all the pieces and get a discount (yes, please), or keep only one or two pieces and return the rest without any hassle. It all starts with filling out a profile on their site, setting a delivery date, and waiting with anticipation.

Catherine

Mesh Laundry Bag Go to your car and dig around for spare change under the car seat until you come up with two dollars and six cents. Then head to Walmart and buy a mesh laundry bag. Go back home and dump every beach toy into it. If you have any bit of OCD tendency in you, then you, too, have done the same. You have sat in some beach condo parking lot at midnight before departure and used the only hose you could find to spray out every speck of sand on each beach toy crevice in sight. You do this mad act while hoping that the sand will not end up in your car, in your one-year-old's diaper, in your minivan's cupholder, and in your soap bar at home. Now your mama beach game will change forever. Simply pack up all the toys in your mesh laundry bag, hose the whole thing down, leave out to dry overnight, and shake it like a maniac in the morning.

NBC's *This Is Us* It is date night and marriage counseling rolled into one. And it's free. It may cost you a box of Kleenex though; my husband cries during every episode . . .

Nicole

Podcasts They're like audiobooks but for people with shorter attention spans. Listening to a podcast while house-cleaning takes all the venom out of rage-vacuuming. *Oh, you don't rage-vacuum? Just me?* I love a good mystery or twelve-part investigation like *Serial*. But currently closest to my heart are *The Popcast with Knox and Jamie*, *The Lazy Genius*, and *The Bible*

Project. The Popcast feels as if I'm listening in on two very opinionated friends having coffee and debating some aspect of pop culture, but I don't have to feel the pressure to join in their witty banter. *The Lazy Genius,* Kendra Adachi, gives me practical tips for things like laundry or shopping at Aldi. She has great taste in books and movies and the tenor of her voice makes me feel immediately at ease. *The Bible Project* and its companion podcast *Exploring My Strange Bible* are both deep (yet accessible) dives into various themes or books of the Bible, but in a very conversational style. My husband and I listen to NPR most mornings while getting ready for work (there's also a treasure trove of great podcasts produced by NPR, but I'll try to reign in my geekery), but when the world feels too bleak and depressing, we'll listen to an episode of *The Bible Project* or *Exploring My Strange Bible.*

***Just Between Us: Mother and Daughter: A No-Stress, No-Rules Journal* by Meredith and Sofia Jacobs** I bought this randomly as a stocking stuffer for my seven-year-old. It wasn't a gift she wanted, but it was the gift we needed. It has questions for mom and daughter, blank pages, and prompts for drawing. She loves writing in it and then discovering what I have written back. Already I have learned she likes snap peas, not that I have ever served snap peas. I also learned her favorite word is *abominable.* She's written about her feelings and her dreams and, because it's in written form, I can respond thoughtfully with all the things I would've wished to say but would've forgotten if she had said them while trying to catch the bus or stalling for bed. Hands down my favorite gift from Christmas.

Acknowledgments

This book is the culmination of the work and dedication of many people, from the contributors to those who helped the final words make it to printed pages. My heartfelt thanks go to:

The inner circle: Cara Johnson, Beka Rickman, and Pamela Wells. It's been an honor. Your hearts and fingerprints are on every page. Maybe don't eat while editing next time, mmmkay?

The eleven contributors, who didn't brand me crazy when I approached them with this hair-brained idea, and then trusted me with their words. I really, really hope it doesn't sound patronizing when I say, *I am so proud of you, sisterfriends.*

Maegan Roper, master of too many things for her own good, whose patience, persistence, and gumption found just the right path for our little book. In this publishing gig, there's nobody I'd rather have at my back. I am blessed to call you friend.

Matt West, our publisher, who wasn't afraid to build a box around our project instead of asking it to fit into one. It has been a pleasure to work with you. Especially the part where I jabbed your bookish sensibilities at the suggestion of defacing this book with a tear-out page.

Lisa Stilwell, whose keen editorial eye and sharp mind smoothed edges and brought forth kindness and true intent. I should probably apologize for scandalizing your Google search history with our references.

Acknowledgments

Brittany Prescott, Regan Kennamer, and Kathryn Notestine of the talented and capable Dexterity team, who helped us build our scrappy little Pinewood derby car, and then made sure the wheels didn't fall off.

Sarah Siegand, EmeraldMade, Kayla Neely, Selena Fettig of BeanPress on Etsy, and Greg Jackson, who wrapped our words in a pretty package, and Alee Anderson, who made sure a lot more moms knew about them.

My husband, David, who makes me laugh every single day. I wonder at your support of me.

And to our bitties, Ellie and Georgia. Keep it rockin', baby-women. Y'all be funny.

Contributors

Abigail Avery

An Alabama native, Abigail Avery appreciates all things fancy and football in equal measure. She is married to the most interesting man in the world (to her at least) and has four adorable kiddos who are mostly well groomed. These are her first published works of any slight or significant interest (absent a law review article from 2006 that garnered at least three readers). She loves old homes, old and new friends, and listening to their stories most of all.

Carrie Brock

Carrie Brock is a mom of three, all adopted in record time and out of birth order. She loves a cup (or two) of black coffee and a good show on the History Channel. She bullet-journals, takes drum lessons, and unapologetically owns *The Fast and the Furious* box set. Her family doesn't look anything like she thought it would, but looks exactly like it should.

Catherine Chestnut

Catherine Chestnut graduated from Wheaton College with a degree in English Writing and is currently residing in Georgia. She married her handsome high school sweetheart and accidentally had four children under the age of four—yes, still recovering from those wonderful "oopsies." She is an INFJ who loves dystopian literature, and a professional volunteer who bakes and exercises in order to bake some more.

Nicole Conrad

Nicole Conrad is probably avoiding grading papers right now. Hopefully, she is playing with her two very emotional and highly energetic girls, Claire and Charlotte. She and her husband are high school sweethearts who grew up in Panama City, Florida: she avoiding activities involving bathing suits, and he wearing a puka shell necklace. She has multiple very important degrees which she uses to shape minds at a Christian high school in Birmingham, where her husband also works.

Emily Dagostin

Emily Dagostin lives in Birmingham with her hunky husband Andrew and two rough-and-tumble little boys. She can usually be found man-venturing with them in the great outdoors, helping them work up an appetite for one of her perfected one-pot meals. Emily enjoys the respite of acrylic painting, Pilates, and reading a good period piece that reminds her of her previous years as an English teacher.

Cara Johnson

Cara Johnson is a Chattanooga, Tennessee native who now lives in Birmingham, where she never anticipated spending most of her life (but is so glad she has). She tries to get outside as often as possible, and is thrilled to have three—soon to be four—kiddos who call her Mom, so she can eat macaroni and cheese weekly without explanation. Before the mac-n-cheese days, she taught high school English for eight years and earned a master's degree in writing, and has since enjoyed freelance writing and editing. She and her best-friend husband dream of a cross-country RV trip with the kids to visit national parks, and wonder what it would feel like to sleep past 5:30 a.m.

Holly Mackle

Holly is the editor of engagingmotherhood.com, an author of the devotional *Engaging Motherhood, Heart Preparation for a Holy Calling,* author of the family Advent devotional *Little Hearts, Prepare Him Room,* and humorist for joegardener.com. In her free time, she enjoys both pop culture and theological podcasts (sometimes back to back), and using every gardening metaphor possible to explain life to her girls. Her bitties want you to know they like glitter, chips, and a ruffled hemline.

Lindsey Murphy

Lindsey Murphy is a wannabe British heroine who wiles her days away sewing, baking, writing, singing, and homeschooling her four most favorite children in the world. She is married to her best friend who sadly does not speak with an Irish accent, but still brings her coffee in bed. If she could live anywhere in the world, it would be Narnia, hands down. You can find her at her online home, lifeabundantly.net, or visiting over at engagingmotherhood.com.

Beka Rickman

Beka Rickman is an avid reader, daydreamer, and optimist. She was born and raised in Southern California, but now resides in the Deep South with her doting husband and three mischievous children. She does not want to go to your big party, however, she would like to hold your hand over cups of coffee and discuss abstract concepts using complex metaphors while laughing at her own jokes. And she does, in fact, enjoy long walks on the beach.

Laura Royal

Laura Royal migrated westward from Atlanta, Georgia and now calls Alabama her home sweet home. She works part-time as a speech pathologist, a job which encourages and humbles her daily. It also serves to give her a place to recuperate from her other job, being the mom to her two daughters. In her spare time she enjoys traveling with her husband, Doug, attempting and then laughing at her failed Pinterest endeavors, and eating anything involving cream cheese.

Caroline Saunders

Caroline Saunders is a writer, advocate of uncoolness, mother to two objectively adorable humans, and wife of an Aaron Rodgers look-alike. She uses her powers convincing her children not to be monsters, influencing women toward Jesus, eating guacamole, and creating a women's retreat experience called Story & Soul Weekend (storyandsoulweekend.com) with her besties. She can be found oversharing at WriterCaroline.com.

Pamela Wells

Pamela Wells is a native Midwestern anglophile currently living in California. She enjoys brewing high-maintenance coffee and trying out new recipes on unsuspecting dinner guests. She has a BS in Nutrition and an MA in Theology, so strangers—apparently struck by pangs of self-inflicted guilt—often put down either their chocolate cake or their wine when introduced to her at a party, to which Pam replies, "Great! More for me!"

Join us online!
Come for the hilarity, stay for the heart.

engagingmotherhood.com   hollymackle.com

 @sameheresisterfriend
#sameHeReSiSteRfRieND

Also by Holly Mackle:

Engaging Motherhood
Heart Preparation for a Holy Calling

Allow your gaze to be lifted from the stifling how-to's
of raising a child onto Christ's sufficiency in meeting
your every need along the way.

Little Hearts, Prepare Him Room
An Advent Devotional That Grows with Your Family

Designed to go deeper as children grow older,
the well-known texts call children and parents alike
to taste the grace of Christmas, and apply that grace
to the parts of life that don't make sense.